LONG LOST FAMILY

Mothers reunited with their sons and daughters; children finally meeting their fathers; siblings brought together for the first time — *Long Lost Family* tells the stories of families brought together after years apart. There's Jennifer, who knew she had a twin sister, but had never seen her — unaware that she lived just a few miles away. Then there's Karen, who discovered her older sister was actually her birth mother, and her search for the father she'd never known. This companion to ITV's TV show reveals the determination to fill the gap in people's lives caused by a decision taken years before . . .

HUMPHREY PRICE

LONG LOST FAMILY

Complete and Unabridged

ULVERSCROFT
Leicester

First published in Great Britain in 2012 by
Headline
London

First Large Print Edition
published 2013
by arrangement with
Headline Publishing Group
London

*A catalogue record for this book is available
from the British Library*

ISBN 978–1–4448–1644–0

Published by
F. A. Thorpe (Publishing)
Anstey, Leicestershire

Set by Words & Graphics Ltd.
Anstey, Leicestershire
Printed and bound in Great Britain by
T. J. International Ltd., Padstow, Cornwall

This book is printed on acid-free paper

Contents

Foreword

I was twenty-nine when I met her. She was the woman who carried me, gave birth to me, spent twelve desperate days with me and then tenderly dressed me in readiness for the social worker's dreaded arrival. She was the woman who attempted in vain to bury the pain of giving two children up for adoption within eighteen months of each other.

I was the cocky young game-show host and DJ — annoyingly confident but deeply needy and, in all honesty, all at sea.

It's a story I have told elsewhere but suffice to say that was the day that I found a mooring. This wasn't a 'new mum' for me. I had the most loving adoptive mum and dad already (and, yes, I call them my 'real' mum and dad) but this was when everything began to make sense.

I didn't know how all over the place I had been until then. I didn't know how much it was troubling me deep inside until I peered at that brand new past and I began to understand so much more about my present and future. Yes, there were more questions, big challenges, but at least there was no longer a deep black hole at the centre of my life. That was the day I began to find myself.

It is not for everyone. Some things are so much better left well alone. It is quite some apple-cart to kick over if you are not ready for it. But for so many, it is the day when the pain finally disappears.

Being involved in *Long Lost Family* has been, without doubt, the greatest privilege of my professional career. To share the news with someone that their mother, son, father or sister is looking for them and then to be with them on the day of reunion and see, hear and feel that raw primal emotion is something that I can barely put into words.

Many's the time Davina and I fell into each other's arms weeping with joy. I know it had the same effect on millions of people watching. Normally I do programmes on controversial issues that make people very angry. What a difference. *Long Lost Family* was quite the absolute opposite. It brought people together and touched everyone who saw it because it made us all think about the bonds of love in our own lives and the stuff that really matters.

I am so proud of these fantastic people. I know the rewards but I know the fear. That meeting is like walking into a parallel universe. It is like finding a completely new past. But it can also be like finding a piece of your heart that has been missing for so long. I know the people who shared their stories inspired thousands more to look and to think about wasting not a second more of our all-too-short time on earth.

Nicky Campbell, December 2011

Introduction

Long Lost Family – The Series

Long Lost Family, presented by Davina McCall and Nicky Campbell, was first broadcast on ITV in April and May 2011. The series, which ran to six episodes, presented twelve stories, every one an emotional journey back into the past — and on to a more hopeful future.

Each of the participants had a compelling urge to track down a missing relative — whether a brother, a sister, a father, a mother, a son — who had been absent from their lives. In some cases, the person missing had gone from their lives right from the moment of birth, and in others, since childhood.

It's been a long road . . .

Many of the participants had been trying to trace their long-lost relatives all their lives. They had each tried to carry out their own searches, scouring archives and electoral rolls, avidly reading any records they could get hold of; some had turned in desperation to private detectives to assist them in their endeavours.

Official files, handed over once the correct paperwork had been completed, would be ceremoniously opened, only to be revealed to be completely empty. One might travel to a small village to knock hopefully on strangers' doors, asking if they knew where the lady who used to live there — but who had long-since moved on — had gone to. All of those hunting for their relatives felt they had reached the end of the line and needed help.

Long Lost Family provided a lifeline to them, opening doors that had been closed before and tracking down family members from all parts of the globe. From the north of England to the sunny suburbs of South Africa and Australia; from villages in South Wales to the sandy shores of the Caribbean; from the heartland of England to the urban sprawl of North America, *Long Lost Family* scoured the world to find answers. Reuniting people who, amazingly, had both been looking for each other, uncovering relationships forgotten about, bringing people back together — *Long Lost Family* answered the questions that had plagued those desperately seeking their loved ones for years.

I can't tell you how lucky I feel . . .

On the way, the programme outlined the

attitudes that forced mothers to give up their babies, or removed brothers and sisters from their siblings' homes. These separations had left a deep and lasting hurt. By handling the complex emotional process of reuniting these people, and in understanding and respecting the difficulties experienced by those who had had to make the heartrending decision to separate their families, *Long Lost Family* sought to bring an end to the years of frustration and anguish felt by those who knew that someone related to them was out there somewhere.

The process of reuniting families was helped not only by a shift in society's opinions regarding unmarried mothers (which also led to the state's introduction of financial support for single-parent families), but also through changes in the law. In 1975 adopted children were given the right to receive copies of their birth certificates, making it possible for the first time for them to trace their birth parents. In the years that followed, a national contact register was established, so that birth parents could list their details so that if their children came looking for them, they would know they wanted to be found. In 2005, after many years of campaigning, the Adoption and Children Act gave parents the opportunity — through registered intermediaries — to look for the children they had given up.

The change in society's attitude to single parents has also had an effect on adoption itself, as has the impact of the 1967 Abortion Act. In 1968, the number of babies adopted was around 27–28,000, and since then the numbers have been in steady decline. By 2010 there were just 2,450 children placed for adoption, only sixty of which were babies under the age of one.

Also significantly affected were Mother and Baby Homes — or, as one in Liverpool named itself, the 'House for Fallen Women.' These were places where expectant mothers could go to give birth and, in most cases, hand over their children for adoption. Not all of them were dismal places and many devoted a great deal of time and care to help these young women. One, in Chester, declared itself 'a long-stay home for young women in need of accommodation and support due to their unfortunate circumstances', with the stated aim of taking 'the unmarried mother away from the tensions of her family circle, from the curiosity of neighbours, or from unsuitable living conditions'. For many of these young women there was no alternative but adoption if their families would not or could not help them: 'I didn't want to give her up, but I accepted that every child should have two parents and I didn't want my child to suffer,' said one mother. Such was the attitude of society towards unmarried mothers at that time that many of those who went into the homes and gave their children away did so because they thought it was the law.

Most of the homes were run by Christian charities, and in some of them the women were treated as if they were sinners. They would be made to work and, when it came to the time to give up their babies, the handing-over rituals could be awful. In one home in the country, the women would push their prams to the end of the drive to the gatehouse, where they would sit in a back room and wait for the adoptive parents to arrive, after which they would return to the home, pushing the empty pram as they went. 'We then went home and lived a pretend life. We had to bury our emotions very deep,' remembered one mother. For some, it could be decades before those feelings could be acknowledged and addressed — and they were the lucky ones.

It's like all my birthdays and Christmases came at once . . .

Long Lost Family presented cases where the resolutions — if not providing everything the participants had wished for during their years of searching — did at least draw a line under unanswered questions and bring clarity to clouded lives. Of course this wasn't always the case, and the programme-makers were sensitive to the emotional turmoil each participant went through. The involvement of experts in the areas of adoption support, search and reunion, and social work was crucial not only in ensuring the programme successfully navigated the complex laws and regulations surrounding adoption, but also in helping the team provide all the emotional and psychological support needed by both the searchers and their relatives.

Ariel Bruce, registered Adoption Support Agency and consultant search specialist to *Long Lost Family*, says the search only represents a small part of the story.

'Sensitivity is crucial. Many traced people are initially shocked to be found and may need as much support as the instigators of the search. The support of an experienced intermediary is of the utmost importance to ensure neither party feels exposed or intimidated by the situation.'

The organisation 'Adults Affected by Adoption — NORCAP', was also involved in supporting the programme, and Jean Milsted, Charity Leader, wrote about the work the organisation does in reuniting families and some of the pitfalls that may await those who are searching. 'Most reunions work well; some wonderfully well, and others well enough. Then there are people who don't want to be found, let alone reunited. When we send out an intermediary letter, we can never predict the response. Some relatives are ecstatic to find the missing piece to their family, but others can be left feeling angry, frightened or upset. To some, it can feel like an unwelcome intrusion. Having buried their losses, digging them up again is just too painful.'

From the stories of single teenage mothers who had to give up their children at birth, to the daughters desperate to be reunited with their fathers, to the women who knew they had brothers and sisters out there somewhere, *Long Lost Family* found a resolution. In some cases, the missing person was on the other side of the world; in others, remarkably, only a few streets away.

For some of those who told their stories during the series, it was a long road travelled. For others, it was a great weight off their shoulders. For each one of them, though, it was a chance to finally discover their own long lost family.

It's like a gift . . .

1

Jennifer, Looking for Her Twin Sister

How I've missed her. Even though I don't know her.

Jennifer Wilson lives in Rotherham with her husband Howard. As a young girl, she lived with her parents and her two older sisters to the north-east of the town, in the area of Eastwood, a few minutes' drive from where she now lives. She grew up feeling cherished and adored, and doubt and uncertainty didn't come into her life. 'My parents were very good, kind and loving. My two sisters were like mothers to me because they were well over twenty years older. We had good holidays, happy, fun days. A smashing family.' Life was a routine of school, tea with her mother and a strong relationship with a lady who lived nearby, whom she called Auntie Eva. Auntie Eva wasn't married and lived just a few doors down with her mother and her son Fred, who was twelve years older than Jennifer.

When Jennifer was eleven, a classmate said

to her, 'Do you know that you're adopted?'

'And I said, 'No, I'm not, no.''

Her classmate repeated, 'You are, and your Auntie Eva, she's your mum.'

'I went home and said to my mum, 'Are you my real mum?' She said, 'Of course I am.''

Jennifer thought for a moment, and said, 'Oh, I thought you were,' and then left it at that. She thought that her school friend must be wrong, and forgot all about it.

Then, two years later, a cousin said the same thing to her. 'She said to me, 'You know your auntie? She's your mum.'

'When I got home after school I said to my mother, 'Is Auntie Eva my mum?' And this time, she sat down and looked at me and said that yes, she was.' Jennifer's cousin had said something else to her too. 'I said to my mum that my cousin had also told me I was a twin. Was that right? Again, she said yes.'

But when Jennifer asked where her twin sister was, her mother didn't know. Curiously, this confirmation didn't upset Jennifer; she took the news in her stride, and focused her mind on the idea that somewhere out there she had a twin sister — it made her feel proud. 'You see things on television where twins are together, and I thought, 'Oh, that might be me one day; I might meet her.'' But beyond that, Jennifer didn't really give it much thought. As for her adoption — nothing more was said, and as a result, Jennifer herself also said nothing. 'The sort of person I am, I don't like any upset; I like everything to be smooth. So it wouldn't have been on my mind to upset either my mum or Auntie Eva.'

With her two sisters being so much older than her, Jennifer was brought up more or less as an only child. She never resented this, although she would have loved a companion to play with and to enjoy every moment of life with her, because she was so well looked after and cherished by her parents. In her mind, being adopted by them had marked her childhood out as something wonderful, even special — she'd been chosen. Still, she knows she would have had more fun with a sibling of the same age. 'I think growing up with a twin sister, or even a sister nearer my age, would have been lovely.' All the activities of her childhood would, she imagined, have been so much more fun for her. 'Going to the coast, on the beach, going swimming, the motorbike scrambles my mum used to take me to.'

There are moments that stand out in her mind. 'Often, on a Sunday, my mum used to take me to the bluebell woods and we would pick the flowers. That would have been exciting, the two of us picking bluebells. And I used to go to Clifton Park, where they had a lot of children's rides that you had to pay for. I used to go on the Cinderella carriage, and it would have been lovely for us both to have gone on it together. And the paddling pool, and the bandstand. There used to be something called Sunshine Corner, which they always said was for children right up to ninety-nine, a little concert with children's entertainment.' Jennifer wondered what it would have been like to have had her twin as her close friend through all of these things. 'It would have been lovely to have had my sister with me, saying, 'They're funny on there, aren't they?' Or, 'They're not very good, are they?'

'I often think of things like that. I used to go to Sunday school, and every year they'd have someone dressed as the May Queen. When I was six, I was one of her attendants. I was in a white dress and it was exciting to follow the queen and walk to the park in a procession. I've often thought, 'I wonder if she's ever done this? What if she was actually there?'

Even though none of the adults in Jennifer's life spoke to her about her twin sister, she did ask Auntie Eva's son Fred, whom she now knew was her brother, what he knew about her twin. It was Fred's wife who told her that she thought she might live not far away, in Wickersley. Even with this information, Jennifer still didn't pursue her by asking more questions of her mother or Auntie Eva. Her nephew Robin, who was the nephew nearest to her in age, said he knew no more than what his mother had told him — that she had been adopted. No one else, it appeared, had her curiosity.

Meanwhile, Auntie Eva was ever-present in Jennifer's life. 'The relationship I had with her was brilliant. We'd go on holiday together, to Bridlington, for a week. That was with my mum and dad as well as Auntie Eva.' At home, Eva was with her almost all the time. 'I'd see her every day because she lived next door but two. She used to come over every night, bringing her knitting with her, and we'd watch television with my mum, just the three of us. I'd go shopping with her every week.'

Jennifer was very close to her; she would even do Auntie Eva's hair. They went abroad together for a holiday. One of Jennifer's older sisters had a villa in Spain, and with her other sister, her mother and Auntie Eva, they were away for three weeks.

In Jennifer's mind, there was never any doubt. 'Obviously my adopted mum was my mum; Eva was just a good auntie. We had a fabulous relationship.'

When Jennifer saw anything about twins on the TV, or if she saw someone with twins in the street, it would prompt her to think about her own twin sister. 'I had a birthday party in our back garden. We put the table out with everything on it — bottles of pop and crisps and sandwiches — and she should have been there. My nephews were there, but my sister should have been with me too.' Moments like that made her wonder: why? Why had they been adopted, when Eva lived so close by? Why had they been split up? (Jennifer was lucky, because many children given up for adoption never even found out that they had a twin brother or sister. If they were not told by their adoptive parents, who themselves might not have been told by the professionals involved in the adoption process, they had no chance of knowing, at least not until the changes in the laws regarding adoption came along. Twins were often separated when the children were given up for adoption as — rightly or wrongly — it was felt that having two babies to look after might be too much for most married couples.)

Jennifer became a teenager, and she started to wonder whether there was anything that she could do to find her. 'I never asked my mother any questions, but I did once ask her where my sister had gone to live, and she told me she didn't know. That was all.' Jennifer did wonder about that, although not at the time. 'She perhaps knew, but she told me she didn't, and what my mum told me, I just accepted.'

The only other information Jennifer managed to get out of her mother was a small hint as to why Eva had given the two girls up for adoption. She told Jennifer that Auntie Eva's mother and father were very old-fashioned, almost Victorian in their morals, although there was also the issue of space. 'They were very strict and Mum said that they'd told Eva that they were sorry but there was no room for two more.' Everyone in the street lived in the same terraced houses, two up and two down. 'I suppose her mum and dad shared a bedroom and Eva and her son Fred shared a bedroom, so there wasn't any room for twins.' If her parents had refused to support her, then Eva had little choice.

That Jennifer had such a happy life at home made all the difference to her, she now believes. If she'd been unhappy, then there was a chance that Jennifer might have wanted to know more about her twin, but as the news hadn't upset her family life at all, she didn't pursue it. She still thought that she would one day bump into her sister, at a dance, or perhaps in town. 'I thought, 'Oh, I bet her mum's told her where I live,' and I expected her to come and knock on my door, and say, 'I'm your sister.' I got it into my head that she'd want to live with me and wouldn't even think about her parents.'

As well as wondering why Eva had given the two of them up, why they were separated and where her sister now lived, Jennifer wishes she had asked her mother why she had adopted her, especially as she already had two grown-up daughters. Of course she could see that what her mother had done was a great thing for her birth mother, Eva, as it meant that she could see one of her daughters every day, even if they didn't live in the same house. Eva was part of her daughter's life and probably helped out with her more than a neighbour normally would. It was a fantastic thing for her mother to have done for her friend, Jennifer knows.

As Jennifer grew older, still nothing was ever said about her adoption. The only times it had been mentioned was when Jennifer had come back from school. 'It was never spoken about again. My sisters never brought it up. Auntie Eva never said, 'Well, you do know that I'm your mum?' Never.'

When Jennifer's mother died, it was the

one time when Jennifer did wonder whether she should ask Eva why she had been adopted. Five years before she died, Eva moved into a home. Every day for those five years Jennifer would go and visit her, but neither one of them raised the subject that was always in Jennifer's mind. She was pretty sure that what her mother had told her about Eva's parents refusing to have her twin girls live in their house was true, but couldn't she have done something about that? Why didn't she fight to keep them? After all, she had kept her son. 'I ought to have said, 'Can you just explain why you couldn't keep twins when you kept Fred?'' And, more urgently now, what did Eva know about her sister's whereabouts? But, in the end, something stopped Jennifer from doing so. 'I thought it would upset her. I just let it lie and carried on as normal.' It's normal for children to think adults should bring up subjects as difficult as this when they need to be talked about, especially when the adults have the answers to the questions that need to be answered, and for Jennifer this feeling had lingered into adulthood. However, now Jennifer thinks that perhaps 'it should have been me who brought it up, because my parents and Eva might have thought that it would upset me. But it wouldn't have.'

When Eva died, Jennifer went to see her at the chapel of rest. She took her daughter Nicole with her. Upset and frustrated, Jennifer said to Eva, 'Why have you died? I need to ask you so many questions, and now it's too late.' She felt very sad about that, as she realised that she had missed the opportunity to ask Eva about the past and the decisions she had made. 'She should have told me. I was old enough to have accepted it and it would have made no difference whatsoever. I felt that my chance had gone.'

Jennifer never felt angry with her auntie Eva when her parents and Eva were alive, because she was so content in her home life and because she always felt she had a good mother and father. But things changed after Eva's death and Jennifer's realisation that she would never know the answer to some of her questions now, questions that had only increased in their intensity over the years. 'I feel angry now. After my mum died, Eva could have explained all this to me and nobody would've been hurt. She could have put me right, hopefully, and at least I would have known — whereas now I don't know anything. I get a bit cross about that. Not because I was adopted, but because my sister and I were split up. I would have liked my mum to have had both of us.'

Jennifer has learned to live with this sense of regret. 'As I've got older, it's bothered me more. It makes me feel sad. When I'm in bed on my own or reading a book, I think about my sister.' She has come to realise that it's not just as a small child or a teenager that she would have liked the closeness and understanding that a twin sister would have provided. 'To have a twin sister now would be lovely; we could go shopping, I could meet her family and I'd be an auntie to her children. We could take it in turns to have Sunday lunch together at my house or her house, and spend Christmas together — we'd have a right good time. Perhaps we'd go on holiday together; that would be lovely because we missed out on that in our younger years.'

As an adult, Jennifer has missed having her sister around on important occasions like her wedding day, but also when she had to have an operation. 'I wonder if my sister's had the same operation, because a lot of twins have similar health issues and have their appendix or their tonsils out at the same time.'

Jennifer wished her sister was beside her during the more difficult times in her life. 'When the miners had the pit strike, my husband Howard was on strike and we couldn't pay our mortgage. I was worried, especially as Nicole was a baby and needed things. Were we going to lose our house? I needed to talk to someone about it, and it would have been nice to have had my sister there then, to discuss with her what we should do. I didn't have anyone to talk to about all this.'

Jennifer's daughter Nicole came later in her life; her husband Howard already had children from his first marriage. When she discovered she was pregnant with Nicole, she went to the doctor, concerned that maybe she was too old to be a mother. 'He said, 'Well, you're only forty-one, so you should be alright.'' It wasn't quite the ringing endorsement she'd been hoping for — and, once again, she really pined to have her sister there, someone of her own age — unlike her other sisters — who would know her well enough to understand how difficult a time this was for her. 'I was worried about whether it would be alright. I would have liked to have been able to discuss it with her, and ask her opinion on whether to have an amniocentesis test. I didn't really have anybody to discuss that with and I felt quite alone because Howard had already suggested that he didn't think it was a good idea to go ahead with it.' They had been struggling with money issues for some time, and Howard was also concerned about the health of the baby.

'I didn't know what to do for the best. Should I go through with not having the baby? And then I thought, 'No, I cannot do that. I've got to have this baby.' I had all the tests and everything came back all clear, but I would have liked to have had my sister's advice and support.'

Jennifer's daughter Nicole has been an important help to her during the times that Jennifer has fretted about not knowing where her twin sister is. 'I never feel like I'm on my own because I've got Nicole, and I can speak to her about anything. But it would just have been nice to have had somebody of my own age to talk to when Nicole had problems or when she was ill.'

As Jennifer settled into middle age, the knowledge that someone more like her than anyone else in the world was out there, somewhere, ate into her heart, every day. She loved her own family, her husband, her daughter, but the pain of knowing she had a twin sister whom she had never seen was something she felt she would never get over. She had to see her, to meet her, to know what she felt — and as the years passed this feeling became more and more intense, to the point where it hurt her to even think about it. 'I wanted to know if she'd had a happy childhood, like I did. What kind of things does she like doing?

Going shopping? We've got a caravan — does she like caravanning? I like to go on cruises; I wondered if she'd been on one? Would she want to see photographs of our mum and our brother? I could show her those.' Every birthday, every Christmas, and on any family occasion, happy or sad, she ached to be with her. 'When we were all sat down at the table, I'd think, 'Why isn't she here with her family?' When my mum died, I thought, 'I wonder if her mum's still living because perhaps her mum was younger than mine?''

* * *

She started her search to find her sister in 1997. She went to Social Services, but the only information they were able to give her, in addition to what she already knew, was that her sister's name when she was born was registered as Judith Walton. However, they appeared to have no records of her adoption. Jennifer believes that both their adoptions were arranged privately by a doctor, and that her grandparents — Eva's mother and father — had a strong hand in the arrangements, to avoid more shame being brought upon their unmarried daughter. The adoption process would still need to have gone to court, of course, to be ratified.

* * *

She also put herself on the Adoptions Contact Register, but there was no information about her sister seeking contact. At a time when no one was encouraged to search for their adopted relative — and there was no legal route to do so anyway — Jennifer felt like all she could do was wait. 'I didn't know what else to do. Social Services said they didn't have enough information and more or less told me I had no chance of finding her. I just didn't think it would be as complicated as this. I expected a knock on the door and 'Hello, I'm here.''

Of course Jennifer didn't know what name her sister went by. Just as her own name was changed from Janet by her mother, did her sister have a new name? And if, as Jennifer expected, she was married, then her surname would have changed too, not once but twice. 'I was stuck; I couldn't go any further because of her name. So when I was checking registers, I'd look for the name Judith Walton, with 'name changed' written underneath and her name now. It was so frustrating because I knew she was out there, but I didn't know where.'

Meanwhile Jennifer always kept alive the hope that she might somehow meet her sister by chance. Whenever she was out and about, Jennifer would imagine that she'd caught sight of her sister. 'If I saw someone who looked like me, I'd hide behind a supermarket shelf and send my husband over to look. She was on my mind every day. I would be out shopping and see somebody with their back to me, with grey hair. I'd automatically think, 'She'll have grey hair.' So I'd walk in front of whoever it was to see if she looked like me, even though I knew there was no guarantee that my sister would look like me. Even on holiday, on a cruise, I'd think, 'Maybe she could be on this same holiday.' I'd see all these people on the decks and I'd think, 'She could be here right now.''

Even when she wasn't keeping an eye out for her sister herself, Jennifer's friends and colleagues often seemed to have spotted her. 'One of my colleagues said to me one day, 'You are stuck up!' I was surprised and asked her why she thought that. She said that she'd seen me in Sheffield the day before and had called over to me. I explained that I hadn't been to Sheffield. 'Oh!' she said. 'Well, whoever I saw, she's the spitting image of you.'' This kind of thing happened often. 'People kept saying, 'I've seen your double today,' and I would tell them, 'Well, I am a twin.''

Once Jennifer took her daughter to hospital for her regular check-up, and the nurse was very friendly. 'She said, 'You used to work here, didn't you?' I said no, and she replied, 'Well, then your double has worked here.''

Another time, Jennifer met Howard outside the hospital in Rotherham, and he said, 'I wish you'd been here, Jen. A lady went past me and if it hadn't have been for the coat she was wearing, I honestly would have thought it was you.'

'I said, 'Oh, you should have run after her and stopped her and asked when she was born!''

Yet another time, a friend of Jennifer's, Elaine, was passing through the village of Ravenfield, just outside Rotherham, with her husband when she thought she saw Jennifer and was about to ask her husband to stop the car when she remembered that Jennifer was away on holiday.

Another incident occurred when Jennifer caught the bus to go into Doncaster. 'The driver said, 'Hello, I've just seen you, haven't I?'

'I said no, and he replied, 'Yes, I have, further up the road.'

'I said, 'No, I've only just got here, unless I've been sleepwalking.'

''Well,' he said, 'you have a double then.''

Jennifer found these incidents encouraging — it meant there was a chance her sister was somewhere in the area.

Eventually Jennifer felt closer in her search. One summer, at the bottom of the road where she and Howard live, there was a beauty school with a visiting clairvoyant. When Jennifer went in to see her, the woman studied her carefully, and said, 'I'm finding this really difficult because there are two of you.' Nobody there knew Jennifer even had a sister. The woman continued, 'Twins?' And she reassured Jennifer, 'You've been trying to find her. Don't worry, you will. Or she'll find you.'

Although she had looked back on her childhood and the main events of her life and wondered if things would have been different with her sister around, Jennifer now wanted to focus on the future. 'If I did find her, we would hopefully have a few good years together, to make up for the years that we missed. I was hoping we'd be very close; that was my wish. I didn't want to just meet her and then that would be it; I wanted us to have a good relationship. That is, of course, if she wanted to be in touch with me. I just hoped she did.'

Thinking about a meeting made Jennifer wonder what her sister was like now. 'I don't know why, but I thought we would be alike. I hoped so. Would we be the same height? Have we got the same colour eyes? Is she the same build as me? Is she slim? I wondered if she had grey hair. Or would she be daring and have spiky hair or a colour on it? And would she be the leader of us two? Which I thought she would be. I like Howard to make the decisions; I go along with the flow. Would she be a bit bossy sometimes, like me? I don't know why, but I thought that we would probably be identical.'

For Jennifer to meet her sister would, she acknowledged, be a strange experience, because she'd given it so much thought already. Would they both dress the same way? Jennifer imagined that if they'd been together as children, they might well have worn the same outfits, and she knows she would have liked that. As adults they might not have dressed the same way, but there's a mischievous streak in Jennifer that thought it would be funny if every now and again they did do so — 'Oh, look, they're twins' people would say, and that would make Jennifer proud.

'It's like torture, having somebody on your mind all the time, knowing there's somebody out there and you just can't find them. Hoping she wasn't abroad. I wanted her to be just down the road.'

When she became a grandmother to twin girls herself, she couldn't stop thinking about why she should have been separated from her own sister. 'When I knew my step-daughter was having twins, I thought how lucky for them both, especially when I found out they were girls. I felt like that could have been us. I've often said to my little granddaughters, 'I've got a twin, but I'm not as fortunate as you two; I didn't live with her.''

Jennifer sees her granddaughters regularly. When they were younger, she and Howard would go to their house while their mother worked. They'd bake cakes together. Howard would video them on walks in the park, the grandchildren holding hands on their way to feed the ducks, or riding their little bikes. Charlotte would chant a constant refrain to her grandmother: 'Where's Becky?' She'd reply, 'She's next to you.'

'I thought that that could have been us when we were little. We could have been having a bath together and baking together and playing with paints and all that. Each time I see my granddaughters it makes me think even more that we should have been together when we were little.'

The frustration Jennifer felt over not knowing anything about her sister boiled over occasionally. 'Whenever I saw something on television about reunited twins, I would think, 'How have they done it?' That really upset me and made me angry.' Part of this stemmed from a fear that she might be too late. 'There was a chance that I would never get to meet her. I hoped she was healthy, like me. I worry a lot. There are a lot of people that I know who have died very young, in their fifties and sixties. I hoped that wasn't the case with my sister.' Jennifer worried that time might be running out for her, although her mother was eighty-six when she died and Eva was ninety-three. 'Hopefully I've got a few years left!'

The other worry that Jennifer had was that her sister might not know that she was adopted, or might not wish to meet a sister she felt no connection to. This reinforced her strong belief that they should not have been separated when they were younger. 'I think twins should be adopted together. I just don't think we should have been separated. She's a part of me, and I'm a part of her; we were born together. When I look at my grandchildren, Charlotte and Rebecca, I see the bond they have with each other, even though they're not identical. That's just how we should have been. Rebecca and Charlotte have done everything together right from the moment they were born. They've got the same interests, the same friends. I'm quite envious of them actually!'

It was through her daughter Nicole that Jennifer was put in touch with *Long Lost Family's* researchers. Nicole was hoping to help her mother find her twin, and posted on an adoption message board that she was searching for someone born during the war, on 24 August, and given the name Judith Walton. Through this, she was contacted by the *Long Lost Family* team, and she put her mother — once she'd returned from holiday — on to them.

Jennifer realised that if her sister didn't know about her, then she wouldn't be looking for her, so she knew that she had to keep trying, in case she was the only one of the two looking. And if she didn't find her, then she had to feel she'd tried her best. 'I would have been satisfied knowing that I had done my bit and tried my hardest to find her. My conscience would have been clear, even though, if I hadn't found her, I would not have felt complete because half of me would still have been missing.'

The desperation Jennifer felt spilled over when she was telling the *Long Lost Family* team about how she felt. 'There isn't a day that goes by that I don't think of her. It just means everything to me, to find her. Everything. I've got a happy marriage, good grandchildren, daughters — but this is just so different. I've got to meet her, I've just got to.'

* * *

The search for her sister seemed like a difficult one — and it would have been near-impossible if it wasn't for the change in the adoption laws that had taken place a few years before. Jennifer had no adoption paperwork for her twin sister and, like many people, had no idea how to go about searching for her. She had a copy of her own birth certificate, which had both her birth name, Janet, and her twin sister's birth name, Judith, on it. But Jennifer had no idea what Judith's name had been changed to after her adoption, and no way of finding out. After the change in the legislation in 2002 and its enactment in 2005, for the first time people were given the legal right to search for family members who had been adopted. This help has to come from specialist agencies, able to access information about an adopted person's identity and then make contact with the adopted person on behalf of the person searching for them. Called Adoption Support Agencies, these professionals seek the consent of the adopted person before they will put them in touch with the searcher.

One hurdle that might have proved difficult to overcome was the suspicion that Jennifer held that their adoption was managed privately, as this might mean there was limited paperwork available to help in the search. However, most private adoptions were legally recognised by the courts. The Adoption Support Agency that worked in cooperation with the *Long Lost Family* team eventually discovered that Judith Walton had been adopted and her name changed to Kathleen. Once that was established, and Kathleen had been traced by the ASA using Birth, Marriage and Death records and the electoral roll, Kathleen was contacted by the professional intermediary who worked alongside the *Long Lost Family* team and told that her sister was looking for her.

Kathleen Millns grew up with her adoptive family as an only child, but she had a very loving and happy upbringing, with lots of friends. She never felt lonely, although as a child and teenager she often wished that she had a brother or sister. When she left school, she went to secretarial college and then went on to work as a secretary, where she met her husband Derek. It was only when they announced their engagement that she learned she had been adopted. They were eating with her parents, getting ready to set out to buy a ring, when her father made the announcement over the table. Kathleen was surprised by the news, but not particularly concerned, and she never felt the need to track down her birth family. Like Jennifer, this was probably because she was happy in her life — and also, of course, because she was busy making preparations for her own marriage. She never asked for any more details, but she assumes that the reason her parents weren't told she had a twin sister — because she can't believe they wouldn't have told her themselves if they'd known — was because it was wartime and certain protocols had changed or seemed less important as a result. Kathleen and Derek have now been married for more than forty years, and they have a son and daughter, as well as grandchildren and great-grandchildren.

When Kathleen received the news that she had a sister, she was surprised and overjoyed. She instantly knew that she wanted to meet her, and told the researchers that this was 'the sort of thing that happens in fairytales'.

The remarkable thing about this discovery, as Nicky Campbell explained when he went to meet Kathleen, is that she was adopted by a couple who lived near Jennifer, in

Rotherham; more than sixty years later, she still lived only three miles from Jennifer's home. Knowing how much Jennifer was pining for this news and a meeting, Nicky was conscious of how powerful these bonds can be — and as yet all Kathleen knew was that Jennifer was her sister. Nicky could only speculate on how she'd feel when she learned that she was a twin.

Kathleen described herself as being on cloud nine when she first received the news. 'I had no idea I had a sister.' She had told her family the news as soon as she'd heard it; Derek, son Richard and his wife Sarah, daughter Julie and her partner Ian were sure that her sister would be older than her, and must have remembered her when she was younger, which was how she knew about her adopted sister. Kathleen wasn't so sure. In the back of her mind, something else came to her. When Nicky went on to explain that one of the reasons Jennifer was so desperate to be in touch with her was because they were twins, Kathleen's response was immediate: 'I knew; don't ask me how. Another one like me — poor old Derek!' The photograph of Jennifer that Nicky showed her astonished Kathleen: 'She is like me, isn't she?'

Jennifer had had years of knowing her family history and that she had a sister, but,

Kathleen had only a handful of days to get used to the idea — and then came the revelation that she was a twin. It took her very much by surprise, and she admitted to feeling 'gobsmacked'. 'This is unbelievable, isn't it? I don't know what to say. I feel I've missed out on a lot. If only she'd found me earlier.' It didn't take long before she started thinking of all the questions she wanted to ask, like whether Jennifer liked sport as much as she did. 'At school, I was involved in everything: netball, rounders, hockey. Or is she the quiet one?'

'Where does she live?' Kathleen asked. It was then that Nicky dropped his bombshell. She couldn't believe it — 'You're joking!' was her initial reaction. But she was thrilled as well as surprised. 'Three miles away, and she's not seen me in Rotherham? She must have, I'm always in Rotherham.'

When Nicky asked Kathleen if she wanted to meet her sister, she said that of course she did. Then she added, 'I've wanted to meet her since . . . I got the letter.'

Nicky said he thought that when she paused she was going to say she'd wanted to meet her all her life. Kathleen gave this sentiment little consideration — 'No, I didn't know she existed, did I?'

Kathleen had to pass on the exciting news

as soon as she could to all her grandchildren and great-grandchildren — Hollie-Beth, Donna (married to Nick, with children Corey and Freya), Shaun (with his partner Rachel and their son Mason) and Rebecca — who were all gathered in the kitchen, waiting to hear her news. To learn not just that their grandmother and great-grandmother had a new sister, a twin sister, but also that she lived so close by made the day an unforgettable one for them all.

When Davina McCall went to see Jennifer to tell her that her sister had been found, Jennifer was over the moon. Her first question was: 'Does she look like me?' Davina said, 'Ridiculously like you,' and when Jennifer saw her sister for the first time in the photograph Davina showed her, she was thrilled. 'Oh, wow! Yes, she does. What a shock!' All the questions and thoughts that had been Jennifer's companions for years bubbled over at this moment, and she rushed to ask another question that had troubled her for so long. 'Is she from round here? Or is she abroad?' At the thought of her living far away, Jennifer's face clouded over and she appeared nervous, awaiting Davina's reply. Davina said to her, 'That's the most amazing part of it; she lives three miles away.'

Jennifer was clearly shocked. 'I can't

believe it! I can't believe it! That's fantastic news.' Looking at the photograph of Kathleen, she declared, 'I can see myself in it.' The happiness she felt was overwhelming, and she threw her hands up in the air, unable to speak for a moment. 'I can't believe it, I can't explain it, I'm just so happy. It's like getting married — you've got somebody else in your life. I feel I could tackle the world today. The one that should be next to me, holding my hand, is here. Oh, I can't wait, I can't! Does she want to meet me?'

Reassured by Davina that she really did want to meet her, and was very excited about the prospect of doing so, Jennifer ran off to tell her daughter Nicole the news. The pair of them jumped about and screamed with joy.

The reunion

Every night during the three-week wait before the day of their meeting, Jennifer read and re-read the card Kathleen had sent her. She kept her photograph propped up beside her bed. 'I still can't believe it; that's why I've been reading this card and looking at her photograph every night.' The photograph fascinated her because, in her sister's face, Jennifer could see herself. She felt she 'knew'

Kathleen — but couldn't decide if that was because she looked like her, or because there was already the intuitive spark between the twins that she'd dreamt of for years.

As she prepared herself for their meeting, Jennifer tried to contain her excitement by wondering what Kathleen was doing at that moment. In part, this was because she knew that in the months and years to come she would always know. These were her last few moments of not having that certainty, and she was relishing the change. What was she going to do when she finally caught sight of her sister? 'Give her a big hug — and a kiss. And just say to her, 'Oh, I have missed you.''

Kathleen was, of course, also preparing herself for the meeting. During the time between finding out she had a twin sister living nearby and the date of the meeting, she had looked hard as she went about her daily routines outdoors. Every likely face was studied, just in case she looked like her sister. She was also excited. 'It still feels like a dream, like it's not really happening.' She knew that this feeling would end when she finally met Jennifer. Naturally she was concerned, but she too was looking forward: 'I'm just hoping that everything works out. I think we've got that bond. We're twins, so we've got to have it, haven't we?'

In both their houses there were two small signs of the changes to come. Kathleen said, 'I can say, 'our Jennifer'' — while Nicole waved her mother off with a cheery, 'Say hi to Auntie Kath!'

The two of them were to meet in Clifton Park in Rotherham, where Jennifer used to play as a girl, and where she always hoped that one day she would be with her sister. Kathleen was to wait for her by the bandstand. On her way there, with Nicky Campbell, she told him that she too had come to play there when she was younger.

Nicky said, 'You don't remember seeing a little girl who looked like you?' At which Kathleen laughed. But as they neared the bandstand, she slowed down. 'I'm so shaky,' she told Nicky. Nicky reminded her that she was on her way to meet her twin sister. 'I am. I'm excited and I'm shaking like mad. Thank you.'

Jennifer, on the other hand, marched towards the bandstand with the impatience of someone who'd waited years for this moment. As the two of them caught sight of one another, Kathleen sprang up from where she'd been sitting and ran to meet Jennifer — the two of them flung their arms around each other and laughed.

Jennifer had brought a little present — but

then she'd thought about her sister's birthday ever since she'd known about her existence. Kathleen reminded her, 'I've only known for a few weeks.' Jennifer's broad smile was a symbol not only of her delight at meeting her sister, but of triumph in making it happen. 'After all these years, I can't believe it.'

They swapped stories. Jennifer explained that although she'd enjoyed some sports at school, she hadn't liked netball, or tennis, making her sister laugh with her comment: 'I always used to pray for rain on Fridays. It never happened.' Kathleen wasn't too impressed when she heard the name their mother had given her. 'I'm not a Judith,' she said, her turn to make her sister laugh. Jennifer told her more about their mother, Eva Walton: 'She was a kind person.' Kathleen wanted to know what Jennifer called her, and Jennifer told her, 'Auntie Eva.'

After their meeting, Jennifer was still euphoric. 'I've always said that I felt like there was somebody beside of me and that something was missing, and I just couldn't explain that to anybody. But right now that funny feeling has gone.' The two of them grinned, and Jennifer added, 'If I'm out shopping and anybody says, 'Are you sisters?' . . . ' — and they both said it at the same time — 'We're twins!' And they laughed, linked arms and walked across the park together.

After the programme

As a thank-you for being involved in the programme, Jennifer and Kathleen were sent flowers, as were all the participants in the series. Bouquets of roses and freesias arrived at both their doors. Jennifer rang Kathleen to say how nice that was, adding, 'Freesias, they're my favourites.' Kathleen said, 'Mine too.'

When the two of them started to compare notes on their lives, the sisters discovered some amazing links. That they had never met before seemed extraordinary now, when they learned they had both been registered with the same doctor and the same dentist for years. How they'd not passed each other in the waiting room, they couldn't guess. Jennifer had worked for years at the Boots in Rotherham's town centre, which was where Kathleen went to collect her prescriptions: 'You must have served me,' she insisted.

Jennifer and Kathleen now meet up at least twice a week. Jennifer and Howard drive past Kathleen and Derek's house on their way into town, so they often call in either on their way there or on the way back.

Since they have been reunited, the two of them have spoken at a twins conference and have been approached to be part of a French TV documentary on twins. They are also taking part in an academic study on twins, which means they have to make regular trips down to London's King's College.

Last year they celebrated their birthday together for the first time. Jennifer's husband Howard said to her, 'The more I look at you, the more I see Kath.' They also share some mannerisms — such as the way they fold their hands when they're sitting down.

There's no point in either of them thinking about the years gone; they're both looking forward now. However, Kathleen has admitted to wondering what it would have been like, as Jennifer used to: 'If Jenni and I had been children together, we would have been double trouble. But we can still make mischief together.'

2

Karen, Who Wants to Find Her Father

'I'm searching for my father because it is a missing part of me. It's something that is not finished and I need to plug that gap.'

Growing up in Leamington, Karen Lloyd had a happy childhood. She lived with her parents, Enid and Jack, and her three sisters, Carolyn, eighteen when Karen was born, Jayne, twelve, and Sally, eight. Karen's early childhood was completely normal, and she grew up knowing she was loved by her parents and adored by her sisters.

Karen's sisters doted on her, and while she wasn't spoilt in material terms, she was lavished with attention and love. Her sisters would ask to look after her, and Karen never felt any resentment from her sisters towards her. If they went out together, they would buy her a treat at the coffee shop in Leamington Spa's town centre. If Carolyn went away, she would always buy Karen a little gift. Once she took Karen on holiday to Wales. 'I just had a very normal, loving childhood,' remembers Karen.

One day, when she was seven, while playing with Sally, looking through a box they both knew contained their dad's important papers, Karen came across her birth certificate. 'I don't even know what my sister and I were looking for, or why we were looking in there.' They'd been told to keep out of the box in case something got misplaced. Perhaps it was the idea that it was forbidden that made it exciting. Sitting in front of the fire with Sally, Karen pulled out the birth certificate.

'I opened it up and read it. At seven years old, I think I did quite well to establish that it was a birth certificate, and I saw some names on there. 'Sally,' I said, 'look, they've got the wrong name on here for my mum. They've got Carolyn's name instead.' Sally looked at the certificate and then looked at me. 'No,' she told me, 'that's right. You're adopted; Carolyn is your mum.''

As soon as Karen realised that Sally was right, she started crying. Sally tried to hush her up and the noise brought their father into the room. He saw Karen clutching the certificate in her hand, and Sally said, 'She found it, and I've told her.' Karen's father stood there and said, 'Oh my God, oh my God. Wait till your mum comes home.'

Later that evening, after a tearful and

traumatic afternoon, Karen was in bed. Her mother went upstairs to soothe her youngest daughter to sleep. 'I remember lying there in the dark, thinking about what had happened, about all that had gone on that day. I just didn't understand why I was not wanted.' When her mother came in, seven-year-old Karen wailed, 'Why did no one want me?' Her mother sat on the bed and fussed with the sheets around her, stroking Karen's hair as she replied, 'Oh, you were very much wanted. You were wanted badly by so many people — that's why you are here.'

For the next few days the atmosphere in the house was unsettled, quite out of the ordinary for the whole family. Those days were hard for them all. In the back of her mind, Karen remembered something else on the certificate. The box where her father's name should have appeared had been completely blank.

When she was older, Karen learned what had happened. Carolyn — Karen has never thought of her as 'mum' as her grandparents have always been her parents to her — had had a relationship with a boy called Peter and had fallen pregnant. Carolyn arranged to meet Peter at Birmingham's New Street Station after she had told him the news, to discuss what the two of them were going to do — but Peter never turned up to meet her. Karen says she imagines that must have been a terrifying moment for Carolyn. 'If that was me in that situation, I'd be so frightened. To have to go home and tell your parents that you're pregnant. It's not like today, when it's not as unusual. In the 1960s an unmarried girl with no boyfriend expecting a baby was frowned upon. She must have been so scared and felt so let down. I can't imagine how devastating that would be.'

Despite his letting Carolyn down so badly, Karen didn't want to be angry with Peter. 'What a terrible thing. Why didn't he even turn up and say, 'I'm not interested'? Why just leave somebody? I think that's wrong,' Karen said, many years later. But she did think he might have had his reasons too. 'He was nineteen years old, he was probably very scared; it's a big responsibility. I wanted to think that's why he did it, that he wasn't a bad person.'

Carolyn went to a nursing home for unmarried mothers. She had decided to have the child and then give her daughter up to be adopted. Just a day or so before she was due to deliver the baby, Carolyn's mother said to her, 'Are you sure that's what you want to do? Because we'll have her; you don't have to do this.' So when Carolyn first laid eyes on new-born Karen and said to her mother, 'I don't want her to go,' the decision was made.

Karen's sisters, Jayne and Sally, hadn't even been aware that Carolyn was pregnant. Carolyn was away, they knew that, but Jayne told Karen years later that the first the two of them knew that something was going on was when their mother came to talk to them. She said, 'I'm going out now, and when I come home I'm bringing a baby back with me.' They were old enough to be completely surprised by this news, well aware of 'where babies come from', but took it in their stride when their mother returned.

As soon as she presented them with their new baby sister, they adored her — and that was that. Karen was their younger sister, and no one said anything about it again. Karen's mother was forty-one when she was born, and her dad fifty. The pair were devoted to their youngest daughter right from the very first day she came home.

Karen had to be formally adopted. This process, Karen was told by her mother in later life, took some time. As part of that, a social worker had to visit them to 'observe family life', in order to ensure that the adoption was a suitable one. Karen's mother told her that whenever the social worker came to call, it was always on the days when Jayne or Sally had their friends round, there were piles of washing and ironing out and the house was noisy and lively. The social worker would sit in a corner and silently watch them all.

By the time Karen was formally adopted, Carolyn had left home and got married. Even though Karen then discovered her true relationship with her 'older sister' at the age of seven, things didn't change between the two of them or between her and her parents. While at first it had seemed something of a novelty to the seven-year-old girl, after a while she put it to the back of her mind, while around her everything went back to as it had been before. For some years, Karen thought no more about it. Jayne and Sally left home and Karen grew up as her parents' treasured youngest daughter, almost an only child.

It was only when the time came for Karen to make choices about which subjects to choose for her O-levels that Carolyn asked to be involved in those decisions. 'There was a big row between my mum and dad and Carolyn and her husband at the time. She was saying, 'I want to be included in this,' and my parents said, 'No, it's up to Karen to decide, and we'll support her in whatever she wants to do.''

When it came to A-level choices a couple

of years later, Karen refused to let Carolyn make them for her. 'At that point, I started to resent it. I didn't think she could just dip in and out when she chose. You're either there or you're not.' Karen had decided her mum and dad would remain just that to her — her mum and dad. That relationship, as far as she was concerned, was not going to change in any way.

'The family I grew up in is my family. It doesn't matter that the people that I thought were my parents ended up being my grandparents. It doesn't change them as people — in my view, it makes them better people. To me, it's normal.' However, there was a question nagging at her. She knew who had brought her up, and that that meant she did not have any problem with her identity. She just didn't know who her natural father was. She only knew his name, Peter Wills, and his date of birth, 25 June 1948.

Throughout her teenage years, whenever there was an opportunity — and those opportunities were infrequent — Karen tried to learn more about him. 'I had questions. Why wasn't I wanted? Why hadn't this man tried to find me? Why wasn't I told before? What else is being kept from me? As time went on, I tried to broach these questions. I'd ask about my father — where he was, what his circumstances had been, that sort of thing.'

Some things Karen felt her family didn't know the answers to, and others she believed they avoided. She now understands that decision: her family felt that Peter Wills had made his choice when he'd left Carolyn in the lurch. They, on the other hand, had acted: they'd kept Karen with them, she'd been adopted to give her a stable background, and she'd lived in a loving and happy home with her mother and father. 'As far as they were concerned, there wasn't anybody else that was my father. The man who I grew up thinking was my dad, to the rest of my family, *was* my dad, and that was it. Why would I need anybody else, when I'd already got my mum and my dad and my sisters?'

Sometimes questions were actively discouraged. Once, when Karen was sixteen, there was an article in the local paper. The journalist interviewed a woman who'd been adopted and had recently discovered her birth parents. Karen's mother, Enid, must have realised that Karen would read it and see similarities in her own situation. 'Did you see that article in the paper?' she said to Karen.

'I knew what she was referring to, so I replied, 'I haven't read it.' She carried on, 'Those things never bring any good, you know. They never bring any good news; it's always bad.' That was all that she said, but I understood well enough; I was to leave well alone and not look into my own past.'

She remained ignorant of her father. Once, her mother said, 'He's not a good person. He's not a person you really want to be involved with, so it's probably not a good idea if we talk about him,' but that was all Karen ever heard from her about him.

When she was eighteen, Karen decided to try to track him down. She knew his name, Peter Wills, and that he'd come from Rugby — Carolyn had told her that much — but little more. She went to Rugby to look through the electoral roll, but could find no trace of him. As her parents were still alive, she didn't pursue her search. Today, Karen says, 'I'm glad I didn't find him then. I wouldn't have been ready for it if I had done, and with my mum and dad alive it would have been very hard on them. I didn't tell my mum I was looking for him because she'd have been really hurt by it. It would have upset them terribly. I was their daughter and it didn't matter to them where I'd come from biologically. I was their daughter, and that was it, from day one. Once they'd died, they wouldn't be there to be hurt anymore.'

As she grew older, though, Karen became more and more determined to uncover the truth. Certain things made it important to her, the most obvious of them all being the birth of her son. When she was pregnant with Rory, she had to fill in a form for the doctor about her family's medical history. In a rare moment of reference to her past, Karen's mum Enid said, 'Well, you'll have to leave that part of the form blank then, won't you?' — and it was the thought that there was a part of her life that was blank to her that drove Karen on.

When her mother and father died, Karen undertook the search in earnest. For the next two decades, on and off, she hunted through records. 'Why isn't he on an electoral roll? He might be in prison for something really terrible. I don't know,' worried Karen. But she had to admit that the opposite might also be true: 'He could be fantastic; he could be a real family man.'

Her husband Matthew would say to her, 'Are you sure you're strong enough to do this at the moment?' What might she find? She had no idea, and no one to ask. 'I don't know what he does, or how good he is, or how bad he is. I just want to know who he is. And who I am. And where I'm from and what I'm made of. At the moment, I don't really know.'

Karen always felt that she was, in many ways, different from her family and, as she grew older, her desire to know where some of those differences came from intensified. 'I'm not vastly different — we're all about the same height, which for girls is quite usual — but facially I'm nothing like Carolyn.' As she grew older, Karen heard little bits and pieces about her father from Carolyn — 'You look like your dad, your eyes, your nose' — but other than that he had dark hair and freckles, she learned nothing else. Not knowing who she looked like, where her features and personality came from, was something she found very difficult to get over. Each of her sisters would say her personality was very different to theirs.

Part of her personality, and maybe something that stems directly from her own past, is that Karen doesn't like to keep secrets, and she doesn't like those she's close to to keep them either. She has never hidden anything from Rory, in the way she feels things were kept from her. Matthew has on occasion planned surprise trips away for the two of them, which sometimes have nearly backfired on him — a weekend in Paris almost brought about the end of their relationship. More comically, a night in Sweden's Ice Hotel got off to a disastrous start when Karen — not knowing where they were travelling to — unpacked to reveal, in temperatures of minus nine, that she'd expectantly put in a bikini.

Everywhere she went, Karen wondered if she would bump into her father. 'I'd look at people and think, 'That could be my dad.'' What would happen if she was in a car accident and had to exchange details with the other driver? What if she had to write down his name and it was her dad's? She would imagine him already in her life without either of them knowing it; maybe he had come to her house to repair a washing-machine, or had stood next to her in the check-out queue at the supermarket. Sometimes, in the cinema, she'd look around before the lights dimmed and wonder if he was there in the room with her.

The image that drove her on was one of loneliness. 'I'd think of him getting older, not knowing he had a daughter. I would have hated to find out I'd started looking for him too late — that he'd died, and I'd never met him. All I wanted was to know who he was — and to see him. If someone had said to me, 'There's your dad, on the other side of the road,' I'd have probably been content. But not knowing was painful.'

There was more. 'Everyone wants a dad. Looking at my own life, and what I value out of life, even though I'm forty-three, it doesn't mean to say that I don't miss having a dad.'

Karen's searches had drawn a blank and she approached the programme-makers because she felt she could go no further. 'For the last twenty years or so, I've dipped in and out of trying to find Peter Wills. I've looked in electoral registers at local libraries, I've gone through phone books, I've trawled various 'find your family' sites on the internet, I've posted things on bulletin boards — I'm looking for this person, he's this age, his birthday is this date. But he may not look at the internet; maybe he doesn't have access to it. I've employed a private investigator to provide me with a list of people of that name around that date of birth. I've even tried calling people with his brother's name and said, 'Do you know Peter Wills?' It's awful making a cold call like that, and sometimes people have asked, 'Why do you want to know?' I've explained that I'm looking for a relative and I've found, to my cost, that became quite emotional for me.'

Karen was in despair. 'There's got to be somebody out there that knows him.'

The research team on *Long Lost Family*, utilising considerably more resources than Karen acting on her own, tracked Peter down, through his brother's family. He was living in Canada, which is why Karen had never been able to find a record of him anywhere. He had emigrated years before, with his wife Angie, and was the proud father of five sons with an ever-increasing number of grandchildren. He had no idea that he had a daughter, and the news delighted him — as well as upset him, as he had to acknowledge that his behaviour in the past hadn't been great. He told Nicky Campbell, 'What an asshole I was!' He readily acknowledged this, with an openness that showed Karen was right to believe in his good side: 'It's bad that I'm sitting here trying to find excuses; it's so easy to do that.'

Peter read out the letter Karen had written to him, which Nicky passed across.

Dear Peter,

I can't actually believe that I'm finally writing this letter to you after forty-three years. I'm sorry if this has all come as a shock to you. I hope that this won't cause you any problems, but now that you know that I exist, you will want to meet me as much as I want to meet you. I grew up in a very loving and caring family . . . I was seven years old when my world was blown apart and I found my birth certificate. I was told that I didn't have a dad, but even at seven years old, I knew I must have had one at some point. I couldn't understand why I wasn't wanted . . . I so desperately wanted to meet you

and put that missing piece into my life.
All my love, Karen

Davina came to see Karen to tell her the news. 'Are you ready for this?' she asked. The tension grew as Karen wiped a tear from the corner of her eye and laughed nervously as she said, 'I think so.' When the news was broken to Karen that her father had been found, she was overwhelmed — 'in bits', as she described later.

Davina asked her, 'How are you feeling?'

'I can't believe it,' Karen replied.

'He wanted you to know that he's always wanted a daughter,' Davina continued.

With the voice of someone who couldn't believe it yet, Karen asked, 'He's pleased?'

'He's not just pleased; he's thrilled.' Davina produced a photo of Peter and said, 'He looks just like you.'

Karen spluttered out, even as she cried, 'I hope not — look at that nose!' But it was true — they did have the same eyes. 'We've even got the same glasses,' she said, trying to laugh through her tears.

Davina had with her a letter that Peter had written in reply to Karen's.

Hi Karen,
On finding out I had a daughter and she had

been looking for me for over twenty years, I was absolutely floored, both with excitement and anxiety. To hear what you went through at the age of seven absolutely killed me . . .

Today I am married to a fantastic woman, Angie, and have been for thirty-three years. We have sons, therefore you have five brothers; they're absolutely terrific and each and every one of them is so looking forward to getting to know you. When I showed your picture to my niece, your cousin, she actually cried, because you are the spitting image of my sister Joan. Karen, I'm going to close here as I cannot see the paper through tears. I hope the day is very close when I'm actually hugging you.

Please don't hit me.

Peter

'That's lovely. He sounds like a really nice, kind man.' Karen hugged Davina and thanked her for bringing the news, the photograph and the letter. The thing she'd been looking for over twenty years — now it was hers.

The reunion

Peter and his wife Angie came over from Canada and he and Karen arranged to meet in the Aviary Coffee Shop, in Jephson

Gardens, a park in Leamington where she used to go often with her dad. Both of them, in their different ways, were nervous. Peter had to ask Angie to help him put his cufflinks on. Even his coat proved troublesome — 'I can't do my bloody buttons up' — because he felt so nervous. When it came to the moment, Nicky Campbell wished him luck and Peter could barely choke out a 'thanks'.

Karen, meanwhile, had enjoyed walking round the park with Davina, but the moment came when she had to walk away from her and go to meet Peter in the café on her own. As she strode away from the group behind her — the TV crew, Davina and her husband Matthew — Karen felt confident, but the confidence drained away with every step she took. Within a short space of time she'd run out of steam altogether and could go no further — it was as if she had walked into a brick wall. Ahead of her was the building where Peter was waiting. She turned and looked back — she could make out the figures far away, watching her, but the only connection she had to them was through the radio mic she had been fitted with, so that the crew could record her words as she met Peter for the first time.

'I felt so alone,' she said, overwhelmed by her emotions and her nervousness. 'I started to cry. What if it all goes wrong? What if he doesn't like me? Even if he does, will his family like me? Am I doing the right thing?' The assistant producer rushed forward with a tissue and a reassuring hug, and somehow Karen found the strength to walk on.

Peter was waiting in the café as Karen approached. She walked past the window as he looked out, and seeing her and noticing the striking resemblance to his side of the family, even down to the wave Karen gave him as she came towards the door, Peter's own nervousness vanished in an instant. 'It's going to be okay,' he thought.

They said hello to each other, they hugged, but there was a silence while they each struggled with their thoughts and emotions. Karen was flabbergasted. She'd waited for a large part of her adult life to get to this point. What should she, could she, say to her father? All she could think as she was looking at him was, 'Oh my God, I look like this man, and I've never looked like another person before.'

'Can you believe this? This is unbelievable, isn't it?' Karen finally managed to blurt out. 'I'm sorry, I can't say anything.'

'Snap,' said Peter. Through tears, he continued, 'God, you've got my sister's eyes.'

'I just can't believe that I've got this great big family that I didn't know I had,' Karen told him.

'You don't know how big,' laughed Peter. 'Why didn't you find me twenty-five years ago?' he asked.

'I didn't know how to find you. I was frightened that you might not want to know me, or that you might have another life — I don't know.' Peter reached out and grasped her hand, kissed it. 'Can't believe it,' she added.

'Nor me,' he said.

'You poor thing, this must be such a shock,' Karen said. Peter hung his head. 'Don't be sad. It doesn't matter, there's nothing I've missed out on. I've had a lovely life, and I'm not angry with anybody. That's life, and things happen.'

'Thank you,' said Peter.

'I'm not angry,' Karen repeated. 'Not with anybody.'

'Thanks,' Peter repeated. 'My life, I can honestly say, is fulfilled. It's absolutely brilliant, unbelievable. Wow.'

'When Peter gave me a hug,' Karen said after the meeting, 'it was really quite safe and strong. It was the way a dad hugs you. That's how it was.'

After the programme

In what felt like a whirlwind to Karen, Peter introduced his family to her. As well as his family in Canada, Peter had two sons living in England. Jason and Antony became good friends with Karen and when Peter returned to Canada she would speak to them regularly. They too had grown up without Peter, although unlike Karen they had always known he was their father and they spent holidays in Canada. Peter would regularly visit the pair of them in England, but Karen felt drawn to them because they too lived far away from Peter. When she spoke to her brothers, Karen would refer to Peter as 'our father, who art in Canada' — which made them all laugh.

Karen, with her husband Matthew and son Rory, went to Canada to spend time with Peter. It was on that trip that she learned more about her father and why he had left Carolyn waiting on the railway platform.

Peter had grown up in a chaotic environment as part of a very large family — his oldest brothers had long left home by the time Peter was born, and he's not even sure of all of their names. Many of those brothers and sisters have since died, and there are only about four of them left out of the dozen or so that Peter recalls. There's a twenty-year age gap between Peter and his older brother Les, and because the family was dispersed, Karen thinks she won't, in the end, get to meet all of her new cousins and uncles and aunts.

At the age of two, Peter was put outside the pub to beg; any money he earned went straight to his father to spend inside. Growing up without a warm, loving and nurturing family was hard for Peter — he had to fend for himself. He had no adult male in his life to show him what was right and wrong, so he discovered life for himself and so has responded to life in that way ever since.

The family were from Birmingham, and Peter spent a lot of time in care there; he lived for a while in a Barnardo's home before being adopted. The adoption wasn't a very successful one for him, as the woman who adopted his sister June only agreed to take him with her when June refused to go without him. But she wasn't kind to him, and Peter ended up back in care.

Peter had several brushes with the law, and in an effort to turn his life around he emigrated to Canada. There he founded a successful business and, with Angie, made a happy family. When the *Long Lost Family* team tracked him down, Peter could remember very little about his time in Leamington.

As a result of meeting Peter, Karen has been able to answer many questions that had been bothering her. Some of them were easier to answer than others. Things such as the traits she had which no one else in her family shared — now she knows where they came from. Her hair, for instance: her dad had blond hair right up until the day he died, aged eighty-two. Peter's hair is white, and Karen's is turning that way. Karen bears a remarkable similarity to Peter's late sister Joan — so much so that Joan's daughter burst into tears on seeing Karen's photograph. Stemming perhaps from her dislike of secrets, Karen regards herself as 'quite good at getting other people to open up', and she thinks she's got this from Peter — 'Peter can talk and talk.' It has given her a lot of pleasure, to recognise where these aspects of her personality have come from.

The harder questions to answer were those that suggested that even if Peter didn't know about Karen, somebody else in the family did. Carolyn had gone to see Peter's sister Joan and asked her whether she would mind if Carolyn gave her daughter the same name as Joan had given her eldest, Karen. Peter honestly doesn't know why he wasn't told about Karen's birth. In the letter that he sent to Karen when he first learned about her from Nicky Campbell, he wrote, 'Unfortunately, at the time that you would have been born, I would not have been a good member of society, and certainly not mature.' Maybe it was for that reason that no one in his family talked to him about Karen, as they thought he wouldn't want to know.

Carolyn told Karen, when Karen discussed her wish that the TV programme would find Peter for her, that she had had a photograph of Peter, but had cut it up in anger when he'd not shown up to meet her — and she regretted that, because she felt Karen had the right to know who her father was and what he looked like. 'I have no problem with you doing this,' Carolyn told Karen, 'because it's only right that you do it. But I don't want anything to do with him at all, whatsoever.' Maybe there were reasons for regret on both sides.

Karen is very happy now to have her relationship with Peter. Although she had a father when she was growing up, she does, when talking to Peter, call him Dad. 'I do think of him as my dad, as he's always been that person, just not in my life. I think that's where I am at the moment; I know he's my dad, but he's not been in my life, although I'm comfortable with him, and he's comfortable with me. And I was comfortable with him right from day one, even that first moment when neither of us knew what to say.'

Now that things have settled down, Karen

can look back and see clearly what a tumultuous time she lived through. 'For a few months we were in a fairytale, and then we came out of that fairytale and stepped back into our own lives.'

3

Wayne, Whose Goal is to Meet His Dad for the First Time

'I look at myself in flashback as a firework that's tethered down, constantly going off; now it's shot up in the sky, it's bursting, it's lovely.'

Wayne Rogers was born into a very loving environment and lived with his mother, father and brother Brett in a village in Nottinghamshire. When Wayne was growing up, he found pleasure in doing all the things that boys do: climbing anything in his way, jumping on his bike to race to the end of the road as fast as he could pedal, running about in the local woods — being active and outdoors was what he loved best. It was when he went inside the house that he didn't feel things were quite right. He loved his mum and dad, but his dad, Pete, didn't seem as enthusiastic as Wayne about what he was getting up to. 'My dad was never into the outdoorsy things.' Wayne's father was academic, and — to Wayne — very English, and he liked things that Wayne didn't really care for, like cricket.

Wayne was always busy and restless — 'I don't sit still.' Filled with this energy, as he grew older, Wayne started to look for an outlet. 'I was constantly at loggerheads with my dad when I was a kid, which created a massive amount of frustration, and that manifested itself in the need for combat.' He had always been fascinated by combat sports, but unlike lots of boys his age, he didn't turn to boxing but to the martial arts. Wayne was involved with the Cubs for a year, but after he had been a member of his local martial arts club for two or three years, he became heavily involved with them instead.

At the age of nine, Wayne started attending regular karate classes — he'd wanted to go from a younger age, but wasn't encouraged to do so. Now he was doing something he enjoyed so much, he found he had little time for anything else. He was deeply serious about what he was doing and worked hard, so much so that he used to train every day. Wayne went on from training hard to taking part in competitions, and the more successful he was, as he moved up the grades, the more he found himself doing, as he started to learn how to teach as well. He picked up some injuries ('I had the end of my finger kicked off once'), but that never put him off. By the time he was twelve, Wayne had progressed to teaching the smaller kids in the club.

When he became a teenager, Wayne became more argumentative at home: 'It's the age-old adage, isn't it? I hit puberty and war started.' The restlessness he'd felt when he was younger affected him more, and he and his dad would disagree on just about everything. 'I'm a forthright character, very different from my dad. We clashed. We're chalk and cheese, basically.' Wayne's frustration at the situation eventually led him to think, 'What do I have in common with my dad?' It seemed to him that they constantly argued, and he felt that they were too different for their relationship to be real. He didn't feel that he was part of his father, or that his father was part of him. 'I love him and I'll always honour him, but there was always that feeling that something was missing.'

Over the next couple of years, Wayne's disaffection with his home life grew stronger and he found himself wondering more and more about his relationship with his father. They shared almost nothing in common, either physically or in terms of personality. Wayne stood at six foot four and towered above his dad, and there was a part of him that had started wondering, 'Am I actually related to him at all?'

'I was getting ready to ask him. I had thought about it because I didn't feel a genetic connection to him. I didn't look like him, I didn't act like him, nothing.'

One summer, when Wayne turned fifteen, he went to visit his uncle Ian in Germany for a holiday. His mother's brother had gone out there when he'd joined the British Army, and he'd met a German woman, married her and stayed. They lived in Bielefeld in northern Germany. Wayne says, 'I was a young fifteen-year-old lad with some money. I'll go to Germany — wow! It was my birthday. It was late and I was tired. I was telling my uncle all about who I was and how I was, and he just turned round and said it.'

'You're just like your dad,' said Ian.

'No I'm not.' Wayne was surprised.

'Yes you are,' his uncle repeated.

'No I'm not,' Wayne responded, more heatedly this time.

His uncle replied, 'You are — your real dad.'

'What he said was the single biggest thing anybody's ever said to me, the most impactful thing. It took my breath away; I couldn't breathe.'

The two of them realised what momentous news this was, not just for Wayne, but also for his whole family. They went off to their beds, and Wayne tried to comprehend what he'd just learned. 'When I found out, it made me feel there was a hole inside me, but I was also relieved by the knowledge. Sometimes I felt angry, sometimes I felt . . . just who am I? Ah — maybe that's why.'

When Wayne woke up the following morning, he felt as if certain aspects of his life finally made sense. Instead of feeling angrier at people like his mother, who hadn't told him the truth, and more frustrated with the life he'd been living, he felt a strange kind of relief. Used to living with confusion and doubt about himself, he was instead slightly liberated by the stunning news. 'I understood everything, all of a sudden.'

Ian's first deed that morning was to speak to Wayne's mother back at home and tell her that he'd let Wayne into the secret. With Wayne beside him, Ian called her at home. When she answered, Ian said, 'I've got something to tell you. It's pretty big, sit down.' When he told her what had happened the night before, the line went dead.

'My mum was angry with Ian, obviously. My mum believed I wasn't going to come back, that I was going to stay in Germany. I did consider it, when I was there. I was just starting my fifth year — I was quite young for my year — but I still thought about getting away, getting a flat in Germany. I'd completed two years of German at school and could speak enough of the language.'

Looking back at himself then, Wayne can see that while he doesn't remember being outwardly angry, he must have been to have considered staying in Germany. 'I was a fifteen-year-old screaming, 'I'm going to fight the whole world.''

In the end, Wayne didn't stay, and when his holiday finished he returned home. When he walked in the front door, he wasn't sure what he'd find. Would anyone sit him down and explain what had happened? Would they try to justify keeping the news from him? In the event, nothing happened. No one said anything to him about it at all. He still loved Pete as his dad, but he now felt that in place of the antagonism between them, which had stemmed, as far as he was concerned, from his ignorance, there was now a gap in Wayne himself, as he felt he didn't know where half of him had come from.

After a couple of days, Wayne asked Pete directly, but Pete didn't want to talk about it. To Wayne, Pete probably thought, 'Wayne, you've got a mum and dad; be happy.' But this wasn't enough for Wayne, who then tried to talk to his mother about it. However, the only details she gave him were sketchy. 'She gave me a little talk about it and told me to leave it alone.' Realising it was painful for his parents, Wayne turned to the rest of his family for help. He found out that as a small boy his surname had been changed to Pete's name, Rogers, when his parents married.

Wayne was told that his mother had had a brief relationship, lasting only a few months, with a boy in the village where she grew up, Newstead, to the north of Nottingham. 'They said, 'Ah, he's a bit wild. Watch out!'' The boy's name was Shaun Freeman.

Wayne's mum became pregnant, and that's when things became really difficult. 'My mum doesn't talk about this very much, which I can understand. I didn't ask very much because I knew it hurt her. But I still needed to know.' There was a bit of tension between the two families, before and after Wayne was born. Shaun was still in the village then, working in the pit, but after six months he left — and never came back. Wayne's mother was then quite ill for a while. She has never liked talking about those times since, and she warned Wayne that if he met Shaun, he wouldn't like what he found. 'It was such a nasty time, knowing that my dad — Pete — wasn't my dad and him never speaking about it.'

Wayne knew he'd only heard one side of the story, but he could never put his mum's warning out of mind. However, with nothing to go on, he tried to ignore it. He continued his martial arts, which remained important to him. The discipline and the tradition appealed to him, especially as other aspects of his life seemed to lack these things. 'Things were happening in my life, and I didn't understand why I was doing them. I was fighting and winning in karate competitions. There was this passion for going against the grain, for fighting. There was an aggression in me. I wasn't fighting in the streets or anything, but I had this passion for combat — for challenge.'

As he grew older, Wayne branched out further. 'I've always been into more exotic things. I was in a goth band, in my mid-to-late teens. I was going on stage covered in make-up, with big chains and spikes all over me. The band was named after an Edgar Allan Poe short story — we based a lot of our writing on his writing. It was all very dark and gothic.' The band was short-lived, however: 'We played a few local gigs, but then we fell apart.'

Wayne was the singer. 'As the frontman, a lot of what I put into it was the show — 'Look at me, I'm showing off here.' I can do a somersault or a backflip in a leather jacket. What I brought to that band was the energy.' The lyrics Wayne contributed to the band's output were, by his own admission, 'quite angry'. He doesn't seem at all disappointed that no material the band recorded has survived, but he's still in touch with the guitarist — 'we're good friends'. However, even the band wasn't enough of an outlet for Wayne's energy and frustration. He still didn't know where this emotion and the drive he felt were coming from. His girlfriend told him one night, 'You need to sort yourself out — you need to find out where this anger, for want of a better term, is coming from.'

At around this time, Wayne registered with a new dentist. It was the first time in his adult life that he'd been presented with a form that asked for his medical history, and he was supposed to give the person who was filling in the form information based on his family's history of heart disease and allergies. Wayne realised that the whole of one side of the form — his biological father's side — would have to remain blank. He felt more than uncomfortable about having to say this. He felt strongly that he didn't want to have to tell these strangers that he didn't know. 'I didn't like this. I had to tell these people that I didn't know where fifty per cent of my biology was from.'

As he entered his twenties, the questions that had bothered him for years started to multiply. 'I haven't got a clue where fifty per cent of my heritage and personality comes from. I do have a short temper. The levels of my aggression are quite scary sometimes, even to myself. I'm monumentally stubborn — that hasn't come from my mum. Where has it come from?' With no one he knew having any real information about his biological father, it seemed as if he might have to forget about finding the answers to these questions. All Wayne had been told were the names of some of his uncles. He would scour the internet, trying to find any trace of a Shaun Freeman in the local area, but there were hundreds, if not thousands, in the county. Every time he searched, he felt as if he were getting further away from his goal. However, Wayne struggled to reconcile himself to believing there was nothing to uncover. 'The major mystery for me was who he was, where he was and what did he turn into.'

Wayne 'cracked on with life, working with bands, running the light shows' before the chance to return to what he'd enjoyed best earlier in life — combat — came along.

In 2007 Wayne went into the British Army,

joining the Household Division, which was based in Windsor. 'It's what I'm all about; it's who I am. It's where I come alive, outside.' Of course he had to go through the same process with the army doctors that he had been through years before with his new dentist. 'I told them I never knew my biological father, which made my family sound bad. I've got arthritis in my foot and leg, which is probably from my martial arts, but I didn't know whether there was a family history of arthritis when the doctors asked me.'

Joining the army brought one thing into sharp focus for Wayne — 'I gained a sense of my own mortality.' And that renewed his determination to find Shaun Freeman. 'When I got the sense, after joining the army, that I could get killed doing this, and I'd never know where part of me comes from — that's when it started getting urgent for me.'

Wayne spent a lot of time, and a lot of money, searching on the internet. He pestered several members of the family, certain that someone had the information he was after. They might not know they had the answers he was seeking, but any clues he could get from them might trigger something in someone else's mind, so he went back to them again and again. 'I was quite forceful. I needed to know. I had to know soon.' Wayne wasted 'hundreds and hundreds of pounds on websites, getting nowhere', but nothing definite or even substantial was uncovered — 'a few more pieces of information, but no definite location'. Whenever Wayne went into Nottingham, he'd look about, in the hope of spotting someone who looked like him, thinking that they might be able to lead him to Shaun. If he saw someone he thought resembled him, tall, red-haired, same strong features, he'd think, 'Should I question them?' But he never did, and no one came up to him and said, 'You look like someone I know.'

After being discharged from the army for medical reasons, Wayne worked as a combat performer in films. 'In *Robin Hood*, when Russell Crowe hands rabbits to a young lad, that's me. Mine's the first Nottingham accent you hear.' He also appeared in *The Eagle*, and was involved in the filming of that even as he approached *Long Lost Family* to ask them to find his father.

It was down to chance that Wayne had found out about *Long Lost Family* at all. 'In the past, I'd never really watch programmes like this, because it would bring back thoughts of wanting to find Shaun, and I couldn't, so it was quite frustrating to watch them. One evening I was surfing the internet, looking for anything that might help me on the sites I usually scanned, and I saw an advert. I thought that it was a chance, but no more. When I later got a phone call from them, I was elated — wow, this is going to happen.'

Shaun remained a mystery to him. Wayne had heard so many bad things about him, but he didn't know what the truth was. 'There is obviously more than one side to every person, and although everything I'd heard about him was bad, I didn't know whether he was actually a good guy deep down inside or not. I knew that I wouldn't know for sure unless I met him.'

Wayne's fiancée, Kez, told the programme, 'If he gets to meet his dad, Wayne will really be able to lay a few things to rest. He just wants to know. DNA can't be changed, but he just wants to know what Shaun's like.'

Wayne wanted to go back into the army and had applied to be re-enlisted into the Grenadier Guards. He would have to undergo medical tests to ensure he was fit enough to be able to join up. The Guards were due to be posted to Afghanistan in a few months. With an uncertain future, Wayne was aware that this might be his last chance to find his father. 'Like many of those who go out to Afghanistan, I wanted to make sure I went out there feeling like a whole person, knowing who and what I was and where I'd come from.'

The *Long Lost Family* team had very little to go on, but among the few facts that Wayne had been able to gather over the years were the names of Shaun's brothers, Kevin, Richard, Mark, Andrew and Simon. The Freemans had left the village where Wayne's mother had lived, and Wayne didn't know where they'd gone. Wayne had no date of birth for Shaun, so the first priority was to find that, because then other records could be correctly sought and identified.

There were hundreds of birth records for the name Shaun Freeman — and they weren't even sure that was the correct spelling of his first name — but they hoped that by identifying his brothers' birth records, maybe that would lead to Shaun. All six records shared one crucial piece of information — their mother's maiden name. A long, painstaking process of cross-checking hundreds of birth records followed, but eventually they had identified all six boys, born in the same area to the same woman. A further check of the records revealed not only her date of birth, but also the date of her marriage to Shaun's father. Combing through the electoral roll, the two of them were found to be living in Nottingham.

The team spoke to them and explained that Shaun's son wanted to make contact. They said they weren't in regular contact with Shaun, that they hadn't seen him for a few years, but that they would be able to get a message to him. Shortly afterwards, Shaun himself called the *Long Lost Family* team.

Shaun had spent most of the past thirty years overseas, travelling and living abroad, but he was now only fifteen minutes' drive away from his son, working as a care worker for adults with learning disabilities.

Shaun relayed his story to Nicky Campbell. He grew up in a small village in the countryside, where he had a simple, sheltered childhood before he met his first proper girlfriend, Wayne's mother — 'Diane was my childhood sweetheart.'

Shaun couldn't remember when he first found out that she was pregnant, but remembered Diane's mother coming round to his house, furious and telling his mum that she didn't want Shaun to have anything to do with her daughter or the baby. 'She was quite a fiery lady,' Shaun recalled. 'She said I was never allowed to have anything to do with Diane.'

Shaun was understandably shell-shocked and terrified to find out that he was about to become a father. He was young and naïve and didn't know what to do. He felt guilt, and was frightened of what his parents would think of him, 'especially in those days. It must have been very, very difficult for Diane as well.' When his mother told him that everything was going to be okay, to leave Diane and her family be, and to get on with his life, he almost felt relieved. 'From that point on, I was not allowed to have anything to do with Diane whatsoever, not allowed to speak to her, which in a village was very difficult. I was already being told to block it out, forget about it, before the baby was born. My parents were just really worried about me getting involved with someone when I was still so young, and didn't want any of us getting hurt.'

Nicky asked if Shaun had ever seen Wayne. 'I saw him once, in a pushchair, in the village. He was six months old. I saw him for two minutes. Not being able to see your own child, even at a very young age, hurts; it really hurts. I tried not to show it because I was told not to. I was told it didn't matter. It does mark you.'

A few months later Shaun left the village and went abroad. He spent many years travelling the world, before marrying twice and settling in the South of France with his wife and children. The traumatic experience of his teens, however, never left him, and he felt in some ways it had very much affected the man he had become and the life he ended up leading. Although Shaun's responsibilities as a husband and father to his other children governed most of his thoughts, he never forgot about the boy he wasn't allowed to father. 'In my mind, he was always there.'

At one point he did go back to the village to try to find out if anyone knew what had happened to Wayne, but nobody could help him. He didn't search further — he felt he couldn't turn up at his son's door and change his world if he wasn't asking for it to be changed. 'What right had I to have any association with him? I'd not been around. I'd not taken care of him. The only association I had as a father was a deed, an act, that had happened all those years ago.' He believed that if Wayne wanted to find his real dad then he would.

Shaun was happy to be found, and happy that Wayne wanted to meet him. 'When I found out Wayne was looking for me, I felt relief. There hasn't been a week that has gone by in thirty-two years without me thinking about him.' However, he was very nervous about what his son would make of him. He was worried that Wayne wouldn't be proud of him. He had no expectations of what Wayne would be like, and just wanted to know that he was happy and had had a good life. He hoped that the experience would give them both a sense of closure, answer questions for them and enable them to put any demons to rest.

Nicky showed Shaun a photograph of Wayne. As so often on *Long Lost Family*, Shaun was surprised and delighted to be able to see the photograph. 'Oh my God, he looks so much like my brother, absolutely incredible. He looks a bit like me actually. Wow.' Nicky had another picture to show him — this time of Wayne in uniform. He told Shaun that he had one to show him of 'Wayne in his work clothes'. Shaun was moved by the photograph: 'Ah, it's in his blood as well. My ancestors have been in the army, they've all done a lot of service — it's one of the roads the Freemans have gone down. Well done, mate.'

Shaun paused for a moment and then observed, 'He's a good lad, ain't he? Look at the size of him!' Nicky told him Wayne's height. 'Six four? I'm six two,' the thought of which made him laugh. Asked if he'd like to meet him, he was swift to reply, 'Yes, of course I do, definitely.'

Davina McCall drove to Wayne's house.

When she broke the news, Wayne was momentarily stunned, and couldn't initially take it in. He had to compose himself for a moment before asking, 'Is he well?' Davina reassured him that he was and offered him a photograph. Wayne studied the picture before he spoke. 'In some ways, it's like looking in a mirror, isn't it? We're very similar.' Later he said, 'I felt elated! We share the same facial structure, the same height.' To Davina, he said, 'Part of me is thinking, 'Why haven't you looked for me? You're not in my life; where have you been?' That in itself does to some degree make me wonder what kind of man he is. If he knows I'm alive, but hasn't looked for me.'

Davina explained to Wayne what Shaun had told them — how he'd thought that wandering into Wayne's life might have been the wrong thing if Wayne knew nothing about him. But she emphasised that Wayne had always been in his thoughts. His reaction was to think for a moment before he said, 'That's intense.' It was all a lot for him to take in — until Davina had come through his door a few moments before, Wayne hadn't known if Shaun was alive or dead. 'That he was alive and well, living in Nottingham, literally minutes from here, took me by surprise.'

Davina passed over the letter Shaun had written.

Dear Wayne,

I would just like to say that I think you are very brave, for going this far to find me. I am sure that there are loads of questions that both of us will benefit greatly from the answers to. You have always been part of my life, and now it seems we will be able to tell people something about our lives. I really can't tell you how that makes me feel after all these years. I am looking forward to our meeting and hope both of us can put to rest certain things that may have been missing up until now. Well, thank you again, Wayne, for creating this chance.

Take care, Shaun

Wayne's first observation was about an issue that had perhaps blocked some of his searches on the internet — Shaun's name. 'That's how he spells it. I would never have known, as there are a few ways to spell it.'

Davina said that what Shaun had written — about Wayne's courage in looking for him and how proud he was — was lovely. Wayne's response was as thoughtful as ever. 'To be very honest, all the stories I've heard haven't painted him in a very good light. But reading this, I don't believe he's a bad person. It's so good to know he's healthy and alive, and happy.'

A smile broke out on his face. 'I can feel a change already. I think I've smiled more in the past ten minutes than I've smiled in a month. I'd like to meet him.' He took the picture to show Kez and her children, waiting in the kitchen to hear the news. After a big hug, he told her, 'I feel so much better. At last, at last.'

The reunion

A week passed before Wayne and Shaun could meet. Apart from the arrangements the *Long Lost Family* team needed to make, there was the small matter of Wayne's commitments — he still had some final moments of filming for *The Eagle* to do. During that week, the issues that had dogged him for many years went round and round in his mind. 'I was still very apprehensive, but I really wanted to go for it.' Working on film sets had taught Wayne a couple of things. One of them was to be patient whenever a camera appeared, as what seemed as if it would take but a few minutes to complete could suddenly stretch out into hours. The other was to appear composed and relaxed when he was in front of a camera. On the prospect of meeting his dad, Wayne said, 'I was more than happy that he was alive, that he was well, to tell the truth. That had been playing on my mind. I don't think I was itching to get on with it. I didn't want to push it.'

When the time came for the two of them to meet, Wayne was unquestionably nervous, but he was looking forward to what the day might bring. When Davina arrived to drive him to the spot outside Newstead where the two of them were to meet, she said, 'What's been the biggest joy for you about finding your father?' Wayne replied instantly. 'Right there, you just said it: finding my father, finding that he is alive.' However, as they approached the edge of the village, Wayne's nervousness took hold. 'I'm slowly running out of words now.' Davina reassured him that, 'You don't need to speak.'

Meanwhile Nicky had gone to collect Shaun. He found him even more nervous than Wayne. 'I don't know if it's fear. It's an emotion I can't describe because I've never felt it before: anticipation, anxiety . . . I don't know. I just want to feel alright, I want things to be alright, I want him to be happy. I want the missing parts to be put together.' When the two of them arrived at the bench where Shaun was to wait for Wayne, Nicky asked

Shaun if he was ready. 'I think so. Ready as I'm ever going to be, after all this time.' As he and Nicky shook hands, the tension he felt revealed itself as he grimaced and said, 'Jesus wept.'

Davina asked Wayne the same question: 'Are you ready?' Wayne's response was almost exactly the same as Shaun's: 'As ready as I'll ever be.' After a nervous chuckle, he added, 'No!' Davina pointed out the way over the playing field and up the hill to where Shaun was waiting to meet him: 'If you walk up there, you can go see your dad. Good luck, Wayne.'

Wayne set off. His journey had to a great extent involved him wondering where the physical side of his heritage came from, and its culmination in this climb up the hill seemed fitting. He felt as if he wanted to race across the field and charge up at top speed. 'Every step took a year off me, and I was going for it. The spring in my step was returning. It felt like I was five and it was Christmas. I was going up to where I had a massive present to open. I could have sprinted up the hill at the time. I wanted to run, I wanted to break into a sprint, but I didn't.' Little of this showed on camera: 'I don't show a lot of emotion, really, when the cameras are on, but that's due to the combat performing — I've trained myself.'

As he got closer, Wayne kept going over the things he was going to say to Shaun. 'I was thinking of all these things to say, that was the problem. That's what I was doing, thinking of all these lines before I met him — and then they'd gone by the time I'd got there.' There was another thing Wayne blamed for his momentary lapse when he got to the top of the hill. 'As soon as I did see him, then nothing would come out. I blame the red shirt for that. I shouldn't have worn the red shirt, a shocking decision that was! I don't think I'll ever get over that. I've got lots of shirts, and I chose a bright-red one.'

Shirt and thinking too hard notwithstanding, when Wayne did reach the bench where Shaun — now standing — was waiting to meet him, he came up with a line that might well have stood for every story in the series, for everyone who'd been searching for their relatives. 'The line was organic; it just happened.'

'It's been a long road,' Wayne said to Shaun, smiling. Each reached out a hand to shake the other's, but then Wayne said, 'Come here,' and they hugged tightly. 'Alright, man?'

'I'm alright,' said Shaun, smiling into his son's eyes. 'What do we do now?'

'Sit down,' said Wayne.

'What a last couple of weeks it has been!' Shaun said, to which Wayne agreed. 'It's always been on my mind really,' Shaun added as he patted Wayne on the back.

'Once again,' said Wayne later, 'I was lost for words. Inside me was a torrent of relief and excitement.' To Shaun, he said, 'I've been thinking about this moment for months and months and months, and when I finally get to meet you . . . nothing's coming out.'

The emotional impact on each of them was powerful, and yet they had each other to support themselves through it. 'I've carried you for thirty-two years, man.' Shaun wept on Wayne's shoulder. 'I didn't know what I'd say. Thank you,' he said. 'If it wasn't for you, we wouldn't be sitting here now.'

Wayne — who was visibly struggling himself by now — took in a deep breath, held it and gestured towards himself. 'Sorry, this is . . . I'm . . . '

'S'alright,' reassured Shaun. They hugged again.

Wayne wanted to make sure that Pete — his dad — was acknowledged on the day. 'You know I've got a dad, and he's a fantastic man, but I can no longer say I've never met my real father because he's sat right in front of me.'

The two of them then agreed to walk back down the hill and go and get a drink. 'You look like me, don't you?' said Wayne.

When they had reached the bottom of the hill and were talking about the experience of meeting each other, Shaun said, 'It's an amazing, amazing feeling, and it shows you that blood is thicker than water, definitely. It's incredible, the way he talks and everything. It's fantastic. I can feel proud; he's a great bloke. I don't know if you can understand what that means. It's fantastic, fantastic,' he added as he wiped some tears away.

Wayne had the chance to do what he'd wanted to do for ages: 'When I finally met him and I shook his hand and I looked into his face and I looked into his eyes, I saw that this man in front of me was a good guy.

'We had the wrap-up in the Railway pub, by the bottom of the hill, with a buffet meal with the crew. We filmed the sign-off shots, then we were done.' Wayne was itching to have some time alone with Shaun, to have the chance to speak to him privately. 'There were things I wanted to ask him; we had places to go.' Once the cameras were off, they headed out into the night — 'We had a right party that night that lasted until three or four in the morning.'

It was an extraordinary evening for both of

them. 'It was like meeting a long-lost friend. We talked about everything. Initially it was questions that would help me get to know myself, but after that it was a getting-to-know-you conversation. The first thing we did was to catch a cab back to his place, where we grabbed his van, and then we came back here to my house, where he was going to leave his van. Having him in my house on that day, that was a lot to take in, but it was good that he met Kez as well.'

Spending those moments together allowed Wayne to spot similarities between them. 'Sometimes, in certain situations, turning off and getting on with the job is what I'm trained to do; Shaun finds himself able to do that as well. Switch off, get on with stuff, turn it back on again.'

After the programme

To Wayne, Pete remains his father, and Wayne won't call anyone else Dad. Shaun understood this and wasted no time in agreeing with Wayne — 'Don't call me Dad because I haven't earned it.' Instead, Wayne calls him Pop — 'my affectionate term for him. It fits him.'

However, if Wayne thought that by meeting

Shaun all the years of wondering about him and what he had inherited from him were over, the following weekend made him think again.

Just a few days after completing the filming for the programme, Wayne had trouble getting in touch with Shaun. Wayne couldn't reach him on the phone at all, as he didn't answer his mobile. A few days later, Shaun got back in touch and came round to see Wayne, who refused to let him into the house, he was so cross. 'Do you realise what you've just done?' he said to Shaun. 'You've put doubt into my mind about everything you've said. You've made me doubt the whole lot.' Shaun was surprised at Wayne's anger and apologised, explaining he had been in Italy for a few days. It was clear that, after the initial excitement of meeting each other for the first time, settling into the routines of their new relationship would take time. Wayne needed to understand that Shaun often travelled abroad, and wasn't going to be around as much as Wayne hoped he would be, just as Shaun needed to understand Wayne's desire to regularly keep in touch.

From a young age, Shaun felt the urge to travel from place to place. When, as a teenager, Shaun left the village he grew up in, he moved to Nottingham to find work and then eventually left the country, only making contact with his family intermittently.

That said, it's clear that events after Wayne's birth played a part in Shaun's decision to leave. Shaun's family life, when he was young, was busy and lively. He says he and his brothers were boisterous lads, no worse than any other lads of that age, and his parents were active members of the local community.

It was after Wayne was born, and the antagonism between the two families developed, that Shaun left — he felt it would be easier for everyone if he did so.

When the two of them were talking and Shaun explained this to him, Wayne realised how close he himself had come to repeating this behaviour when he'd been on holiday in Germany and first learned of Shaun's existence. For a brief moment, Wayne had considered not returning home, running away from the world he knew. 'Looking back, that's exactly what Shaun did. He left to go and live with his brother, and not long after he left to travel around the world.'

Shaun settled in France, where he raised a family. That was one of the first discoveries Wayne made when he and Shaun talked on that first night — that he had a French half-brother and sister — and only a few months later they came to visit Shaun in Nottingham. 'It was nice to know that,' Wayne said. Wayne also learned that there was another son living in Nottingham, but he's not met him yet. It made him a little uncomfortable, as it brought back memories of the emotions that he had had about Shaun before he met him. 'Alright, so there's another one out there: who is he? What's he like? Is he like me?' It also explained something that had happened occasionally to Wayne in the past. 'My friends occasionally said to me, 'I saw you in town the other day' — so maybe, what with me and Shaun looking alike, they'd seen him.'

The hunt for Shaun — the need for Wayne to understand his background and all that comes with it, like physical resemblance and personality traits, as well as the wider interconnected links of cousins and uncles and aunts — had dominated Wayne's life to such an extent that not only was Kez keen for Wayne to find some answers, but his mother was too, as she knew it was something Wayne needed. 'I had to do it. It was affecting me, my family, my fiancée and the children, because I knew that sooner or later I was going to go back to work, back to the army, and I could go off to war and be killed — and never know. Never knowing was a big thing for me. It had to happen — I just had to do it. Family, family lines and family history are very important to me.'

Since Wayne met Shaun, there's been a noticeable change in him. 'Kez says I'm more relaxed and calmer. Before, even if I had my feet up, the things that were most important to me would come back into my mind. Now I don't have that anymore. A lot of questions were answered. The anger and frustration that has fuelled me for years isn't there now. Before, I was impatient with myself. Those emotions, those feelings, become imprinted on your personality. What's there instead now is a sense of oneness with myself. I don't need to prove myself anymore. I can stand up proud and say, 'I am me,' and be completely convinced about that.'

Part of that change came from Wayne's decisions both before and after he met Shaun. Right up until the moment Wayne met Shaun, he remained quite angry with him, and was waiting to meet him before he decided if he could forgive him. 'Then we spoke, and I knew he was telling me the truth.' It was this sense of trust that gave Wayne a new way of looking at himself, and that came as a surprise to him. 'It's very strange; I do feel that genetic connection with Shaun.'

The conversations between the two of them revealed more things that Wayne hadn't been aware of, but which others seemed to know. For instance, Wayne's grandparents — whom he hadn't met — lived not far from the place Wayne had first heard about, Newstead. It seemed a lot of his relatives knew this, but no one had thought to mention it to him. Wayne's not sure why this should be, but assumes that maybe no one else felt his sense of urgency — the drive that pushed him on — and thought things would be better left to work themselves out. 'I'm a little bit upset with my family about that. No one really told me anything because my father's family were seen as troublemakers by my family. Also, no one knew how they'd react if I turned up and announced I was his son. It would've been heartbreaking if I'd been cast out.'

Finding these new relatives has been an extraordinary experience for Wayne. For a start, he now has contact with family who are, or were, in the army — one of whom, he believes, was in the Grenadier Guards. 'I can't trace him yet, so I said to Shaun, 'If you ever talk to your dad about him, let me know.''

Wayne met most of Shaun's relatives when Wayne's grandmother — whom he had not met — died and Shaun invited Wayne to the funeral. 'It was there that I met most of my cousins and uncles.' The event didn't start in the most auspicious way, as, when Shaun walked in with Wayne alongside him, there was a moment straight out of an old Western. 'Everything went quiet. Oh dear! There were hundreds in there, and they all knew I was coming, they knew who I was. They knew everything about me, as they'd all watched the programme. It was very unnerving. I've worked on film sets, I've been in films, I've stood in front of hundreds of people and sung, but that was perhaps the most unnerving thing I've ever done.' Wayne looked round the room, saw all the faces turned toward him and said, 'Hi folks, I'm Wayne,' after which Shaun said, 'Right, do you want a drink?' and they walked to the bar, with Wayne half expecting a piano to start up in the background, like it would in a Western saloon.

After a few moments, everyone came up to talk to Wayne. 'Now I've got two sides to my family, like everyone else,' he says. 'That was one hell of a day — I won't forget that in a hurry.' Wayne met his five uncles and many of his cousins — 'I fit straight in because I'm so like them.' Opportunities like that allow him to observe Shaun, and he can see how similar they are in so many ways: 'When I talk to him, it is like being in front of a mirror. Our smiles are similar, as is the way we construct sentences.'

As their relationship has grown, Wayne has learned more about Shaun's travels abroad. It's amazed him to realise that if he joins the Grenadier Guards and is sent to Afghanistan, he'll be going to a country that Shaun has already visited. Of course when Shaun travelled there, it was safer, something Wayne wishes he could have experienced. Shaun has told him a lot about the place.

Now that Wayne's met his father, he can work out which traits he's inherited from his mother and which ones come from Shaun. 'I have a few traits from my mum, the major one of which is probably my temper. I am quite quick to lose my temper if provoked, and my mum is the same. Shaun can have a temper, apparently, although I've never seen it. My willingness to party, I get from my mum — she's a partygoer, although she doesn't like to drink. I don't drink much now because if I do it can become a routine. I only smoke a pipe, not cigarettes, because I know you can get addicted very quickly. My mum never had that, and I wanted to know where that came from.'

Shaun is very personable, very easy-going, and he gets on well with people — Wayne envies him that. 'Sometimes I find it easy to get on with people and have a laugh; sometimes I find myself being very private.' But since Wayne met Shaun, that's changed. 'In the past I would be quite stand-offish. I'm less so now. In a lot of ways, I feel that Shaun has awoken that in me. He has unlocked the potential that has always been in me, and that is very liberating.'

Wayne still hasn't worked out where his interest in combat comes from. His fascination with martial arts isn't something he shares with Shaun, although Shaun's 'very spiritual' and that is part of the martial arts too. In the absence of anything more concrete, Wayne's decided this side of his personality comes 'from a mix of Freeman and Jackson genes'.

Shaun's wandering nature is something else that Wayne envies. He too would like the opportunity to travel, but he doesn't have the freedom that Shaun has. Wayne's career goal at the moment is to return to the army.

Wayne doesn't envy everything about that freedom, though; that's not in his nature. 'I like to know what's happening, when it's happening, how it's happening. I'm more controlled.'

There's no doubt that the experience of meeting Shaun has changed Wayne dramatically, but that's in part because Wayne 'allowed it to. I believed that when I met Shaun things were going to start making more sense for me. I believed that to such an extent that consequently they did. Having things fall into place, having questions answered, helped me to understand myself. Now I understand myself in greater detail than I did before, I'm able to give myself much more fulfilling challenges.'

His experience of being on *Long Lost Family* was entirely positive for him because he prepared himself for it and decided that he would benefit from it in advance. However, if things hadn't gone quite so swimmingly with Shaun, Wayne still feels he would have made some progress in himself. 'I still would have understood a few things. When I'd got these boots laced properly, I could make them march, as is said in the army.'

Ever since he was a young lad of fifteen and learned of Shaun's existence from his uncle Ian in Germany, Wayne struggled to understand himself. 'Why was I less academic and more physical when I was growing up? I've never been one for maths. I may have A-level chemistry — I can do the maths for that — but not basic-level maths.' In part, he was assisted by the psychologists that each participant on *Long Lost Family* saw before they went ahead with making the programme.

They helped Wayne put things into place, 'which is why I'm quite comfortable talking about things now. In the past, I didn't like talking about things, and I was quite frustrated with that aspect of my life.' Wayne was told that he was fighting against everything simply because he was fighting in his own heart, all the time. 'I should have realised it myself; I've got a psychology qualification.' At the time, Wayne didn't realise how fundamental these insights would prove to be once he met Shaun, but looking back he can see how invaluable the process was for him.

Appearing on the programme has also meant that Wayne has been approached by several people who tell him that they too would like to find their fathers. Some of them are people he's worked with for a long time, some are strangers, and they all say, 'You've inspired me to find my father.'

Obviously Wayne's aim at the moment is to return to the army, but in the meantime he's keeping busy teaching martial arts to kids as well as to army cadets. When he has time, he and Shaun get together — if the weather's nice, they'll pop down to the canal to go fishing. Otherwise they play on the Xbox, shoot the breeze and generally enjoy each other's company. 'There are times when we're both thinking, 'Should we go out?' There'll be a sly look in his eyes; we both know what we're thinking. We'll get permission and off we'll go. Sometimes we'll mark the occasion, do something of note.' One such occasion was Wayne's birthday, when he had a barbecue at his home. Once he'd established that his mum and dad weren't going to come along for the day, Shaun was invited. Shaun came, bringing a lovely Bonsai tree, and everyone had a good time. At one point in the afternoon, he and Wayne slipped indoors and had a moment alone, just the two of them. It meant a lot to Wayne to be able to see Shaun on his birthday, in his own home, and Shaun obviously relished the occasion also, clapping his arm on Wayne's shoulder and saying, 'You're one now. I've known you for one year; you're one.'

What was normal for Wayne — his anger — has gone. 'I believe all that energy just gets changed. Nothing goes away. That anger has now been channelled, and I don't want that frustration ever to return in any shape or form. I'm much more of a rounded person now, much more settled, ready to take on life and whatever it throws at me.' If Wayne gets his place in the Grenadier Guards, then one of the things that will be thrown at him will be a posting to Afghanistan. 'If I do go to

Afghanistan, now that I've found Shaun, at least I can go with a solid mind. I can go focused. Its what I've trained for, it's my job. It's a different feeling, going off on tour, I'm protecting my country, my mates, getting the job done.'

With the anger gone from his life, does Wayne think he has less of an edge than he used to? 'As a combatant — not only in life, but in the martial arts — there isn't the edge that the frustration gave me. Now I'm more of a teacher, an instructor. I can see that frustration and anger bubbling away in another young person. I can see the direction he or she needs, because that's the direction I needed, and I can help them because I can understand that feeling. Now I've calmed down, settled down, teaching others is the direction I want to go in. Anger and frustration has been replaced with a resolution and a calmness and stillness that only a resolution can bring. I've transformed the anger into energy I can use to help others with.'

Wayne has taken stock of himself and the transference of that anger — and why it didn't come between him and Shaun. 'I could have taken the anger that was bubbling inside me and used it. I could have met Shaun, smacked him, chucked him down that hill. It did go through my mind — 'What happens if you meet him and all of a sudden — snap?' The human mind's quite capable of doing that, and its only a fine line between that and totally flipping out. That went through my mind, but there's too much self-control in here for that to be able to happen.'

But there is something else. I've never been angry with Shaun, truly angry with him. I've never felt a deep aggression towards him for not being there, not being part of my life, because I wouldn't be the man I am today without Pete. And that's what my mum and dad have done for me — helped me to evolve into the person I am now, which I don't think is a bad one — I get on with life in my own way. Sometimes I think that if Shaun had been there, I may have turned out differently, more nomadic; I may have been influenced to explore the world. My army career would probably never have taken off, because I would have taken Shaun's ethics on board.'

Wayne is clear in his mind about the division between his dad — Pete — and Shaun. He stresses that he is the man he is today because of his parents. 'I call Pete my dad and Shaun my father. Pete is my dad and I love him to bits. I couldn't have asked for a better dad. Shaun is my blood, and now that I know him, I'm a lot calmer.' Wayne has asked the questions, and found the information he has sought only for himself, and not with any intention to hurt Pete or his mother in any way. 'I love my dad Pete. I think he's a fantastic man, and he'd have to have been to have put up with me. I was a bit of a nightmare. I never broke the law as a teenager, but I was always running my life at the speed of light. Always.'

That restlessness hasn't completely left him. Wayne does want to travel and see the world — a desire that got a boost when he met Shaun and talked about his life. 'Then I understood why I've always had the desire to move on. Knowing that, now I can control that desire. As soon as I know something, I can control it. There's always been that wanting to run — always. The allure of travel — of going out and seeing this rock we live on — its something I'm passionate about.'

4

Debbie, Hoping to Find Her Son

'For some stupid reason I got it into my head that his birthday would be the day he might knock on the door. I don't know why, but I used to think, 'He's going to come and see me today.''

Debbie lives in the little village of Westbury-sub-Mendip in Somerset with her husband Brian. She has recently started working for NHS Direct. When she was younger, though, at the age of nineteen, she was more unsettled than she is now. She and her first husband Paul had a very young son, Daniel, but their relationship was rocky and they separated. 'We both got married young and there were lots of problems,' said Debbie. 'I was very insecure; I was all over the place.' Living in Dorset at the time, she went to work as a barmaid in the Three Choughs in Blandford.

Blandford Forum is a town with a long history, but it is its proximity to a large army camp that provides the town with much of its income. The Three Choughs was no different and many soldiers came to drink there. 'This guy came into the bar where I was working. He was tall, good-looking, he knew all the right things to say. He was the only black guy who ever came into the pub, which made him even more mysterious and interesting. I was totally bowled over by this guy showing me so much attention, and I fell for him — hook, line and sinker.

'There was a split in the town between the squaddies and the townspeople as it was. It's a funny little town.' As there were only about three black soldiers in the entire camp, anyone who associated with one of them was noticed, and Debbie came up against a lot of prejudice. 'I got a lot of flak. Some girls waited in the toilet for me one night, when I was closing up, and gave me a bit of a beating. One day I went into the local supermarket and this girl on the deli counter refused to serve me, using the most insulting words she could think of.' Even members of her own family didn't want Debbie seeing him.

Vulnerable following the separation from her husband and flattered by this man, 'Things happened very fast. I thought he was interested in me, but looking back on it, he wasn't — he thought very highly of himself and not so highly of others.' Through the winter months, the two of them were often together; he'd come to the pub when she was working, or he'd go to her home and she'd cook them both a meal. Sometimes he'd come round after he'd been to the pub or a nightclub — there weren't many opportunities for the two of them to be seen out on their own.

When Debbie realised she was pregnant, he didn't want to know. 'I was so scared. I knew it was going to be difficult to tell him, and when I did he just didn't want to know, he didn't care, and he told me to get rid of it. It was just a complete inconvenience to him. I didn't see him again until I was very heavily pregnant, and when he saw me, he crossed over the road. I never saw or heard from him again.'

Things were further complicated by the fact that Debbie was not entirely sure that he was the father, as she had also been seeing Paul. When she and Paul decided to give their marriage another try they talked about what might happen if the baby wasn't Paul's. 'He knew all along that there was a really huge chance that the baby wasn't his, and we decided that if it wasn't, we would look at adoption. But there was always that little chance that maybe it was Paul's baby.'

Debbie clung to this slender hope throughout her pregnancy, but it was a very difficult time for her. 'Going through that pregnancy, knowing that there was a chance that I wouldn't be able to keep my baby — that was a horrible feeling, to be honest with you.'

* * *

Eventually she went into hospital in Dorchester and gave birth. 'I had quite a difficult and long labour, longer than I had with my first baby. I think a lot of that was because I wanted to hold him in. As long as he was there, it was going to be okay; he was still mine!'

Her son was born, and he was very fair-skinned. 'I fed him straight away, even though I was quite poorly — I'd had to have a blood transfusion. They asked if I wanted him in the nursery or in the room with me, and I asked for him to stay with me because I was over the moon — everything was alright, I was able to keep my baby, and I didn't have to make tough choices or anything like that.' Paul had seen the boy and Debbie and then stepped out to ring Debbie's mum in London, to tell her that Debbie was okay — not great, but okay — and that the baby was theirs. Debbie's mother sent a card and flowers straight away. 'I was told he was my husband's baby and everything was fine. So I breastfed him, and I had him with me for the first day and night.'

The next day the paediatrician came round to check the baby. His manner, Debbie recalls, was abrupt. He didn't seem to show any feeling towards her as he looked the baby over. 'I remember him checking him over, taking his nappy off. Where the skin was creased, he could see it was dark, and he said, 'You do realise' — those were his exact words — 'You do realise this baby's mixed race?'' Debbie and Paul were stunned. There was silence for a moment, and then Paul spoke. He turned to the nurse by the cot and said to her, 'Can you take him out of here?'

The baby was wheeled away to the nursery, and Debbie cried and cried. 'I couldn't stop crying, it was awful, and I cried until Paul left, four or five hours later.' At that point a nurse came in. 'She was a lovely West Indian nurse. I was still in a terrible state, and she was so nice and quite motherly, and she said, 'Now you listen here, Debbie. If you don't stop this crying, they're going to put you on a psychiatric ward. You need to get yourself together now, come on.' She was calm and considerate in her manner to her patient, after probably the worst few hours of Debbie's life, and that helped Debbie to stop weeping. The nurse then said, 'Would you like me to take you to see him now?'

'She took me down to the nursery. I was in hospital for another four days and whenever my husband wasn't there I'd go and sit with my baby. Whenever I could, I'd be with him — I called him David at the time.'

During those four days, Debbie was visited by a social worker. The notion of sending David to a foster mother had been discussed with the social worker before the baby's birth. 'She came to see me in hospital a couple of times, now that David was born, and asked, 'Are you happy for that to happen?' I wasn't. I asked my husband if we could take him home, and he replied, 'No, Debbie, you've got to be realistic.''

Paul was coming to the hospital as often as he could to see her — not only did he have to work, he was also looking after their son Daniel. Then came the time when Debbie had to leave the hospital and go home, while her new son stayed behind. 'I had to leave him at the hospital, and they were going to take him to the foster mother, Mrs Fudge.' At the time, Debbie was too distressed to see any humour in her name — given that her own surname was Cake.

As she was still unwell, Paul drove Debbie to her mother's house in Bexleyheath. Throughout the journey, Debbie felt as if her world was tearing apart. 'I thought my heart was going to break. I don't know what I'd have done if I hadn't had Daniel — he was the only thing that stopped me from going over the edge.'

Debbie was still very poorly, and while she was at her mother's house, she had another bad haemorrhage. Being physically ill made her even more unhappy, as she could barely move. 'I remember lying on the double bed at my mum's feeling absolutely awful — because I was no longer feeding him, I'd get quite a lot of discomfort. Lying there, all I could think about was, 'I want my baby, I want to feed him, I want to be able to cuddle him, I want him with me.'' This longing went deep inside her, driven by her body's natural processes after giving birth. 'All the while I was thinking, making plans in my head: 'What can I do? How can I get my baby back?' That's all I could do, make these plans of how I was going to sort all this out so I had Daniel, and Daniel had his father there, and I had my new baby.'

Debbie had willing accomplices in her planning. 'My mum, my older sister Sandra and my auntie, who was staying with my mum — the whole family were aware of what was going on. Most of my family were very, very supportive. There was talk — because I was in such an emotional state and looking for any way that I could keep David — we talked about Mum adopting him, and that was great. But then we discussed it further, and Mum said, 'Look, I'm sorry, but it would be unfair on him and unfair on Daniel to do that.' On reflection, yes, that would have been quite a cruel way of doing it. My sister, bless her, then said, 'I'm going to adopt him. We'll sort it out.' But she wasn't married at the time, so her situation would have made it very difficult for her to offer David a home.

After Debbie had recovered sufficiently to return home, she went back to Daniel and Paul. Ten days had passed, and David was now with the foster mother, Mrs Fudge. 'Sandra — I couldn't drive at the time — would come over when Paul was at work and we would go over and spend time with him there.' Sandra became very attached to him as well, and she and Debbie would talk about the possibility of David coming home with them one day. Debbie said to her, 'He's a little baby — how could Paul not love him?'

Eventually she rang the social worker and told her, 'I've been thinking, I want to have him home with me.' She said the same to Paul, and he was prepared to accept this, as he could see what it meant to Debbie. All the arrangements were made, and David came to their home. 'Paul did try, he did. In fact he couldn't have tried any harder. David was home with us for nearly three weeks, and he said he was a lovely little chap. He'd feed him, play with him and change him. When I saw that, I'd think, 'Oh, this is going to be okay; he wants him' — but he couldn't accept him, although he was never horrible to him.'

One night, after David had been home with them for two weeks, Debbie came up to the bedroom where Paul had changed David and prepared him for bed. 'I went in and smiled, and said, 'He's lovely, isn't he?' And Paul said, 'He is. He's a gorgeous little lad, he really is, but he's not mine and I can't . . . ''

David went back to Mrs Fudge's, to await the next stage: adoption. This was the most difficult decision of Debbie's life. She had to decide whether she should keep David, in which case Paul would leave, or whether she should forget her own feelings and attempt to do the best for both her sons, by keeping Daniel in a stable home with his father, while ensuring David was given a similar life with another family. 'If I had kept David, I would have been a single mum with Daniel and David, in a small town, where there would have been some real prejudice going on. I don't think I was strong enough or mature enough to give him the love and support he needed.'

Debbie worked closely with a social worker to find David a good home. Events moved very fast, and within a fortnight of David going back to Mrs Fudge's, Debbie, who'd been looking at profiles of prospective parents, found herself going with the social worker and her son Daniel to a sports club's pavilion, just outside Blandford, where she was to meet a couple who seemed ideal. Debbie had said to the social worker that she wanted David to go to a family where he would fit in, so she'd rejected a Chinese-English couple ('I said no, explained specifically what I wanted, ideally a black father and white mother') in favour of an American couple, Dona and Jerry. The couple already had a six-year-old daughter of their own, but were unable to have any more, and Debbie had asked if she could meet them.

When they arrived, the couple were there already, and Debbie and the social worker went in, with Daniel in his pushchair. The social worker announced that she'd leave them to get on with their conversation, if the three of them were comfortable enough with each other. 'They were very welcoming and we got on very well,' said Debbie. Jerry, Debbie realised, was an officer in the US Air Force. 'Jerry was a very nice man. He stood up the whole time, talking to me and to Daniel, so I guessed he was in the military. He was quite a tall guy as well.'

He told Debbie he was based in the UK for the moment, but they would be going back to the US. 'We sat and talked. It helped having Daniel there, a little child for them to chat to. They asked me questions about myself and my background. I struggled for a while, as my emotions were all over the place. I was frightened, but I was really curious to meet these people and make my decision. I felt very quickly that they would be the ones, but I wanted to talk to them for a while to be sure. I wanted to know lots about them, so I asked them questions too, but they were not allowed to give me answers to some of the things I asked. I only knew their first names — I assumed they knew my full name, but as it turned out, they didn't — and they had been told they weren't allowed to tell me which part of America they came from. They said they had to be careful what they said.'

Debbie made a point of watching them talking to Daniel, seeing what sort of rapport they could strike up with a very small child — Daniel was just over one — and how they behaved with him. They told Debbie about their own daughter, and explained that they couldn't have any more children. 'She was very grateful. She kept saying, 'I can't believe that you'd consider doing this for us.'' All the time she was there, Debbie knew that what she was was doing the right thing — but she couldn't help wanting to grab Daniel and run right out of there, to go back to David and keep him with her. 'All I wanted to do was to run away from the whole thing. I never wanted to give him away. I wanted to hold on to him forever. It was difficult because I already had a child and a marriage, and I had to do the next best thing and find someone that would love him.'

Jerry and Dona promised Debbie that they would love and look after David, and, because they were so lovely, she believed them. They told her that when he was of an age to understand, they would tell him about his mother and give him a letter from her. They had one request to make of her: could they change the boy's name to Jonathan? Debbie had named her son David Mark. Dona and Jerry renamed him Jonathan David Marc.

Debbie was parted from baby David, and he went to live with his new family. 'To me, he's always been my son, and always will be.'

Some years after she had given her son up, her marriage to Paul ended in divorce. Debbie remarried and changed her surname.

In all the years since his adoption, Debbie has never kept David a secret — she felt it would have seemed as if she was ashamed of him, when nothing could be further from the truth. If she was ever asked, she would say, 'I have three sons. Two live with me, but unfortunately I had to give one up for adoption.' Her sons, Daniel and his younger brother Ben, knew since they were tiny that they had a brother who lived in America. There wasn't a day that went by when Debbie didn't think about her boy, and she remembered the promise about the letter made to her, and wondered.

When it came to his eighteenth birthday, she started looking out for him, expecting, almost, to hear a knock on the door. When she didn't hear from him, she started to imagine things: her worst fears were either that he wasn't given her letter, or he'd read it and wanted nothing to do with her. 'Mum used to say to me, 'You've got to take something good from that, because he's happy if he hasn't tried to find you. That means he's happy. You've got to accept that.''

Each year Debbie would mark his birthday, even though she no longer bought him a card — which she'd done for each of his first five birthdays. It was a day she always found especially hard, and those around her became used to her being withdrawn and unhappy on that day. 'My boys were always aware when it was his birthday. When he was about seven, Ben was sitting on the bed, and I said, 'What's wrong? You look sad.' And he said, sighing, 'Yes, I am sad. I'm just thinking about my brother; it's his birthday soon.' I never forgot that — he never said anything like that again, but that one day he just came out with it.'

Debbie started searching for her son when she knew he was approaching his twentieth birthday. 'My main route was always the internet. I'd put in his name, Dona and Jerry's names, whatever I could.' She put his name up on internet message boards, on adoption forums and on the official registers in the UK. She listed his date of birth, the name of the hospital, and she even mentioned that David would have a sister and that she believed he was somewhere in America, even though she wasn't certain of that, thinking that with Jerry's job he could be anywhere in the world. 'I felt I was coming to a dead end.' She spoke to someone about placing her name on registers in the United States, but just as she was contemplating doing so, she learned about the *Long Lost Family* programme, and contacted them instead.

Debbie now lives with Brian, who has also

always known about her son and has always supported any efforts of hers in searching for him. Debbie is an Elvis fan, and in 2008 she went with her mother on a tour of the southern US, visiting places familiar to any Elvis lover. 'We went to Atlanta, Tupelo, Graceland, New Orleans, where we spent three days, and Nashville. We were in a shopping mall near Nashville, and I said to Mum, 'My son could be any of these people. America's a big country — but we don't know for sure that he couldn't be, do we?'

When she was asked on *Long Lost Family* what she would like to say to her son, Debbie said, 'I hope he understands how much I love him and loved him, and will always love him. I hope that letter conveyed that. He never did anything to deserve this. I want to know that he's been happy; I so want to know that he's had a good life. And I want to ask him not to hate me. To give me a chance to explain.'

The Adoption Support Agency working with the *Long Lost Family* team were allowed access to the adoption records, thanks to the change in the law a few years before, and this meant they could find out Debbie's son's adopted name. Armed with that, it wasn't long before they were able to track him down, in Arizona. David Cake was now known as Jonathan David Sledge. When the programme contacted him to say they were searching for him on behalf of his birth mother, Jonathan was over the moon — he was thrilled to be found. He had searched for many years for Debbie and had almost given up hope that he would one day meet her.

After being adopted by Dona and Jerry, Jonathan lived in England until he was two years old. With Jerry in the air force, the family moved around a lot, and Jonathan lived all over the world — California, Japan, Hawaii, San Diego, Washington — before finally settling down. He lives in Arizona with his wife Rachel and their son Jordan. Dona and Jerry divorced, but he has a good relationship with both of his parents and told the programme-makers that he had had a happy upbringing.

Nicky Campbell went to meet Jonathan, who showed him the folder he had kept for years, about his birth mother. 'My mum told me about my birth mum, and that she wanted to keep me and love me, and gave me her letter.'

> I think this is the hardest letter I've ever written. I feel I must tell you how much David means to me. I know I can never forget him.

Jonathan wasn't given the letter until his

parents thought it was the right time for him to read it. 'I was fourteen or fifteen, and it took me hours. I wanted to read every detail of it. It was the only thing I had from my birth mum.'

When Jonathan was growing up, he thought about his birth mother often. 'I thought about what she was like, what she was doing.' He wondered what it would be like to meet her: 'You always imagine some big reunion, but in reality you don't know what it's going to be like.' But he was so pleased to hear that she'd come looking for him — and that she had been looking for him for so long. 'That means that she cares, she must want to know about me. It's made me a lot happier to know that every feeling I've had about her has been mutual.'

Nicky was intrigued to learn that Jonathan had been searching for her as well, and that he'd been searching for her for so long — 'on and off for ten years now'. Of course Jonathan had been searching for Debbie under her previous name — Debbie Cake — because someone had once let slip to Dona and Jerry about the oddity of Mrs Cake visiting Mrs Fudge. Debbie had always assumed they had known her surname; it turned out they had, but only from this chance remark. Not knowing her new surname meant Jonathan had never had any luck in his search. Despite the length of time he'd been looking for her, Jonathan was never worried that he might not meet Debbie, and his only regret is that — when he learned that Debbie had been looking for him for a long time too — 'It's just sad, really, that all this time's gone by.'

One of the questions that Nicky asked was how Jonathan felt about Debbie. 'I don't have any anger. I've never had that feeling.' Jonathan had wondered if maybe she didn't want to try to find him because she was now in a situation where she could no longer acknowledge him. 'I thought at times that she wouldn't want to meet me. I didn't know what family she had now, whether I was a secret.' Nicky reassured him that he was never a secret in her life, and that everyone who knew her also knew about him. He added that while Jonathan had wondered if she was interested in knowing about him, Debbie too had thought maybe Jonathan didn't want to know her.

Nicky gave Jonathan a photo of Debbie, which brought a big smile to his face. 'It's good to see her finally. It's so much at once — twenty-six years of nothing and then all this happens at once.' Asked how he felt about meeting her, Jonathan was adamant:

'Yup. I just want to know what was, what could have been, what can be.'

After Nicky left, Jonathan drove over to see Dona and his sister. They were both excited for Jonathan, as they'd known he was searching for Debbie. Dona said to him, 'I think this is really exciting for her to have found you. I think I've waited your entire life for this day,' at which point she became very emotional, 'because I wanted to fulfil my promise to your birth mother. She gave me a beautiful son, her most precious. And so the next step will be . . . ' and she paused ' . . . to check our passports.'

In London, at a hotel, Debbie met with Davina McCall and told her her story, that she was very young when she'd had her baby and how difficult those days had been. Debbie found Davina to be a very sympathetic listener, and she told her how important it had been to her that her son was adopted by a couple she felt would look after him well, and she spoke about how much it had helped her that both Jerry and Dona were open and fair in the way they responded to her. 'It sounds silly to say, but at that point it seemed like Dona was a friend. She didn't seem to judge me, and she said she'd never forget that I'd given her this chance to have another child.'

At this point Davina surprised Debbie by telling her that her son had been found, that his name was Jonathan David Sledge, and that he lived in Arizona. Of course Debbie was astonished and delighted and wept with sheer happiness. 'Is he happy?' was her first question, and Davina comforted her by saying, 'He's really happy.' Her next question was about his family. 'Have they looked after him well?'

'Really, really well.' At this point Davina produced a photograph but, she warned Debbie, 'Before I show you, I want to let you know something really important. That he's not angry with you, and he doesn't hate you.' Davina knew that one of Debbie's fears was that Jonathan didn't want to be in touch with her — after she'd not heard from him, even though she'd written him that letter — because he was angry with her. Even after hearing Davina say this, she still couldn't believe it: 'He doesn't feel rejected at all?' Davina insisted that he didn't.

When she finally saw the photograph of her son, the breath that she'd been holding in tightly escaped from her. 'Oh, oh my God, he's absolutely perfect.' Through her tears, she broke into a smile. Davina explained what an enormous thing this was for Jonathan, because 'he's been looking for you'. This news was even more of a surprise for Debbie. 'Oh, you're joking!'

Davina added, 'I don't think he'll really believe it until he meets you.'

Debbie was stunned. 'Does he want to meet me? Do you think he will?'

Davina was delighted to tell her, 'I think he'd love to meet you, if you want to meet him.' It was clear that this, for Debbie, was never in doubt.

Davina then handed Debbie the letter Jonathan had written to her.

Mother,

I have been trying to write this letter for days. My whole life I have imagined what you were like and what you were doing. I have always wondered if you thought about me as I thought about you. When I was fifteen, I read the letter that you wrote. Since then, I've been looking for you with not much success. I have always been afraid of finding you and you not wanting to know me. I am excited to meet you and to find out where I come from. Thank you for finding me. Maybe now I can feel whole.

Reading the letter aloud choked Debbie up. She turned, overwhelmed with emotion, to Davina and said, 'He wants to see me.

Thank you,' and the two of them hugged tightly.

Afterwards Debbie rang her family and told them the news. They were all, like her, over the moon, especially her two sons, who couldn't wait for the opportunity to meet him. Her eldest, Daniel, was so excited that his brother had been found that he insisted Debbie take a picture of the photo she'd been given with her phone and send it to him right away — and he rang straight back after she'd done so, shocked at how alike he was to Jonathan.

'My biggest fear was that he'd died,' Debbie said. 'Now I know every day that he's okay, and where he is.'

The reunion

The meeting between the two of them was arranged for the middle of January. Just a few days beforehand, Debbie and Brian were married. The day before the meeting was due to take place, Debbie was visited by the *Long Lost Family* team — but it nearly didn't happen. 'On the Wednesday before the meeting on Friday, I felt awful at work. I was burning up. The film crew were due the next day, to film some shots they needed to use as background. I was genuinely unwell, and my voice went.' The team urged her to go to the doctor, who suggested that the only way of getting her voice back was to rest it — not an option right then. 'We might have to postpone the meeting' was a suggestion immediately overruled by Debbie. Brian said that her whispery voice added to the effect anyway, and so everything went ahead as planned. (It took four weeks for Debbie's voice to return. When Debbie went to the US to stay with Jonathan, she said to him, 'This is my real voice — and this is how much I actually talk!')

The meeting was to take place in Dorchester, in a park 'a stone's throw from the hospital where Jonathan was born'. Debbie still found it difficult to think of him as Jonathan, as did her mother: 'My mum still can't call him Jonathan. I'm getting used to it, although in my heart he's David, but my mum refers to him as David because all these years we've talked about David. We've kept him alive, and he's always been David in our lives.'

In addition to losing her voice, Debbie had recently had an operation on her back, which meant that earlier on in the filming she had had to use a walking stick to assist her in standing; now she walked with a limp as she slowly healed. But nothing would have stopped her from meeting her son that day. As Brian said, 'Today is majorly important to her. When she gave Jonathan up twenty-six years ago, she always wanted to get back in contact with him, and she's been looking since he was eighteen years old.'

Debbie added, 'I've carried this love for years, ever since he was born, and I just worry about how he's going to feel today.'

Both Jonathan and Debbie had been told by the team and the adoption experts working alongside them to take the reunion slowly and not to be too ready to rush ahead: 'We were both told to just see how it went. I told them that the rest of the family wanted to meet him, but again they said no, that we should take it easy to begin with. It was strange that both of us were asking the same things.' This advice from the experts was only sensible; if things hadn't worked out, then to have set too much store on the meeting and what it would mean for both of them might have caused more problems later on.

Jonathan had flown in with his whole family — his sister, mother, step-father, his wife and their son. Dona observed that 'He is such a nervous wreck. He may say and he may look like he's together and calm, but he's not — he's just shaking inside. I just know that his stomach is torn up.'

Jonathan himself was wondering how it was going to go: 'I'm just trying to think about what I'm going to say, and haven't figured it out, but at the same time I'm just waiting for it to happen. Let what happens happen.' Nicky Campbell asked him how he was feeling — was he feeling good, and had he thought of what he was going to say to his birth mother? 'Yes,' Jonathan replied to the first question. To the second, he said, 'No, I tried to, but I'm just going to let what happens happen.'

Debbie was asked to sit on a bench to wait for Jonathan to arrive. Every second of waiting to catch sight of her son for the first time in decades seemed like an eternity to her, and her tension was only made worse by the effects of the operation she'd recently undergone. Davina remained very supportive: 'She was lovely, she was great. She is extremely warm and caring, and she shows a genuine interest in you.'

Eventually Jonathan appeared at the top of the path. Debbie was amazed at how like other members of her family he seemed, even at that distance. When he reached her — and Debbie did have to restrain herself from jumping up to go to him — they threw their arms around each other. 'My lovely boy,' she sobbed into his shoulder. 'How are you?' They looked into each other's faces.

'Good,' he said, crying too.

'Nervous?'

'Yeah.'

'Thank you for not hating me,' she said to him. 'You don't know how much that means to me. May I hug you again?' Jonathan was so moved he could barely speak.

'I just wanted to touch him like a mother would,' Debbie said afterwards, 'and just hold him, and he totally felt like he was mine, my son.'

Jonathan added, 'I was hoping for the best, that she would be welcoming, but I didn't know what to expect . . . But then it was all just so emotional. It was great.'

For Debbie, there was a bonus to their meeting. 'I've carried so much guilt, for so many years. To suddenly know that you don't have to feel like that anymore is something . . . it's like a gift.'

After the programme

The next few hours and days were extraordinary for both of them. Each of them learned a lot about what had led them there that day, and Debbie was able to thank Dona and Jerry (the latter via Jonathan) for what they had done for Jonathan. It turned out that it was Jerry who had sat Jonathan down at the age of fifteen and handed him the letter Debbie had written, desperate and unhappy, all those years before. 'I've thanked him, since I've met Jonathan, as the person that gave him the letter. They always promised they'd give him my letter, and Jerry did. From then, Jonathan wanted to find me.'

Hearing about that letter again reminded Debbie of how difficult for her those days had been. The restrictions imposed by the law at the time meant that Debbie was not allowed to know Dona and Jerry's surname ('I'd found that hard, as if I couldn't be trusted, even though I was giving them my son'), and, after Debbie remarried, nor did they know hers. This made it difficult for them to do what they wanted to do, which was to keep in touch with her and make sure she always knew how Jonathan was. As he grew up, Dona sent regular letters with photographs to the social worker who'd assisted with the adoption, hoping they might be passed on to Debbie, but as the law then restricted contact between the parties involved, the letters were not passed on.

Jonathan had a folder all about Debbie, with the letter she'd written to him and all the notes he'd made as he searched for her. He knew — from the slip someone had made — that Debbie's surname was Cake, so he had listed all the Debbie Cakes he could find in Europe on the internet and approached each one of them. One had moved to Australia; another was dead. When that path led him nowhere, he listed all the Cakes in the UK and started working his way through them too. After a while, he found that dispiriting and called a halt to the task. He showed Brian and Debbie the list. 'Look here,' said Brian, 'just three names below where you stopped is Debbie's ex. If you'd contacted him, he would definitely have given you Debbie's mobile number.'

There was more. When he'd been approached by *Long Lost Family*, it was explained to him that as Debbie and Brian were getting married, the reunion would have to take place after that date. This was too tempting for him, and, fired up with excitement, he went back to the internet and — this time — came across one of Debbie's messages on a bulletin board. 'I became your stalker,' he told her, as he did everything he could to find out about her.

As soon as the cameras had been packed away after their initial meeting, Jonathan and Debbie headed back to the hotel where Brian and her sons and their partners were waiting to meet them. Jonathan's family came too, and the mass reunion 'was amazing'. Jonathan's son Jordan met his cousins George and baby Austin. Later on that evening they all went out for a meal together, and then the next day they set off down to Bournemouth, to go and visit Debbie's mum. The following day Debbie's sister Sandra — who was also desperate to meet Jonathan, but who had been unable to drive down the night before — arrived to spend the day with them.

While they were travelling around, the group went on the chain link ferry to the Isle of Purbeck. On the ferry, the three brothers got out of their cars and went up on deck with Debbie, where they had their photograph taken. They returned to their cars, and Debbie turned to Brian as she got back in. 'I never, ever thought I'd do that. I've just had my photo taken with my three sons together, and I never thought that would ever happen for me, that I'd be able to say that.' That photo meant so much to Debbie.

They arranged to return to Debbie and Brian's home in Somerset. The original plan had been to return their hired car and spend the night in London, but Debbie and Brian had suggested they change this arrangement, return the car to Heathrow and spend as much time as possible with the family. Jonathan expressed a desire to visit a castle while they were in England, so the party stopped off at Corfe Castle on the way — and then fitted in a quick glimpse of Stonehenge. Debbie made chilli and a macaroni cheese for dinner that evening.

Debbie told Jonathan that she'd imagined he might be in the shopping centre outside Nashville that she'd visited in 2008, and she even asked if he had been there at the time — but she knew that he hadn't been. 'I think I would have known him, if he'd been in that shopping centre. He was my boy.'

Everyone was exhausted, finding that the exhilaration of the occasion made them even more tired when they finally went to bed. The following morning was chaotic, as those returning to the US rushed about packing bags and generally getting ready to depart. Thinking that no one would have time for a proper breakfast, Debbie made a heap of bacon and egg rolls and placed them out, with some bagels, for everyone to help themselves. Jonathan took one and disappeared into the room next door.

Later, when he'd returned to his home in Arizona, he told Debbie why he'd had to go out of the room — he'd been eating the roll with tears pouring down his face. Everything about the weekend had been magical for him, and the dinner that Debbie had prepared the night before had a huge significance for him. He said to Debbie that he was sorry that he'd wandered off, but he'd been thinking about what could have been — and, more happily, what the future would bring.

They travelled up to Heathrow together, and Debbie and Brian waved them through until they couldn't see them anymore.

After years of having to explain to people that she had three sons but only two lived with her, Debbie was now able to say exactly where Jonathan was, what he did and when she would be seeing him next. For Daniel and Ben, it was the same: after years of knowing about their brother, he was now fully in their lives. All of them started making plans for the next time they would see each other, but for now, they relied on email, Facebook and the telephone to get them through it.

Debbie returned to work, and proudly produced her pile of photographs. 'Here's my son Jonathan. Here he is with his brothers. Here's one of me with Jonathan. Here he is with my mother.' Everyone was happy to look at them until someone ventured, 'Er, Debbie, didn't you get married too? Haven't you got any wedding pictures?'

As soon as the programme was aired,

Debbie began to be recognised. The day after it was shown, she took her niece and grandson to an adventure park. 'It was embarrassing, people coming up saying, 'You were that lady on telly last night. Oh, I cried with you last night.' I felt myself go so red.' Later on she and Brian went to do their shopping at the local supermarket. A man walked past them a few times, staring at Debbie, before he walked over to his wife and said, loudly enough for them to hear, 'Yes, it is her.' Brian waited till they went past again and said, 'Yes it is her from the telly,' to them. Meanwhile Debbie was approached by another man and his wife. He became very emotional as he explained that he had been adopted and that he was desperate to try to find his birth mum. Debbie gave him the best advice she could — and she has stayed in touch with his wife, offering to help in any way she can.

A week later the two of them were due to fly out to stay with Jonathan and Rachel. As they stepped on to the bus, a man looked at Debbie for a few moments before saying, 'Oh, you're the lady who was on telly a few days ago, aren't you?'

'I was able to tell him that we were just about to fly out to see my son.' The same happened in the airport terminal, where person after person stopped either Debbie or Brian and asked after her and Jonathan. All of them wished the couple good luck on the trip. They were tired out by all the well-wishers even before they got on the plane. 'We thought that once we'd got to America, it would be nice and quiet, as nobody would have seen it.'

When Brian and Debbie suggested they hire a car, Jonathan said, 'I'm going to drive you around; I'm going to show you everything.' Debbie and Brian stayed with Jonathan and Rachel and their son, Jordan, two years old, was fascinated by his new visitors, Nana E and Papa Ian — he couldn't pronounce Debbie and Brian. Their fortnight over there was a fabulous time for all of them, even though Jonathan and Debbie burned the midnight oil every night. Brian and Rachel would head to their respective beds at eleven o'clock, leaving Debbie and Jonathan talking till four in the morning. 'We'd talk about the pertinent things, but then we'd talk about religion, politics and everything. We were getting into some really interesting discussions. He's very much like his brothers, delving into unusual things.'

One conversation that was difficult for Debbie was when Jonathan said that there was a part of him that wished that instead of giving him up for adoption, Debbie had just waited, because her marriage had later broken up. He understood that she'd had no choice in the circumstances, and that she'd had no idea how her future would turn out, but he couldn't help feeling that way. (Ben, Debbie's youngest son, said, when he heard this, 'Well, you wouldn't have had me then, Mum!')

Jonathan took time off work while they were there, and he and Rachel treated Debbie and Brian to an amazing surprise. As a birthday treat for Debbie, they took them to Las Vegas for three days, to see the Elvis show, with the hotel paid for and VIP seats for the show. 'I still can't get over it. What have I ever done to deserve having something so lovely,' said Debbie. 'The two of them put so much thought into it.'

On the drive to Las Vegas, they drove past the Joshua trees made famous by U2. If Debbie thought this would be the only connection back to the UK, she was wrong.

'We were in one of those eat-all-you-want buffet places, and I'd gone up to get my plate while Jonathan was still sat at the table. When I sat back down this lady came over and said, in an English accent, 'It is you, isn't it? I was just looking at your handsome son and thinking he looked like the man who was on telly the other night, and when you came over I realised it was him, and that you were together!' '

Debbie and Brian cringed, but for Jonathan it was a marvellous moment: 'I'm famous!' he kept saying. The series hadn't been screened in the US, but after thinking for a moment, he worked it out: 'There's probably about three or four thousand British people in Las Vegas. Let's say about forty per cent of those people watched the programme, so to them, I'm well-known!' To Rachel and Brian he joked, 'Of course you two only had bit parts; we're the stars.'

That wasn't the end of it. 'The next day we were on the Strip, and the same lady came up again. 'Hello!' she said. 'Do you know, I feel like we're related now. I feel I know you so well.' Jonathan was grinning widely, as if to say, this is great! And then, at the Elvis show, a couple wouldn't stop looking at me and Jonathan. I said, 'Keep your head down' and Jonathan said, 'What do you expect when you're famous?' '

When they'd returned to Phoenix, Debbie told Jonathan that she was piecing together her family tree and wondered if he'd like to see what she'd done so far. She was worried that it would bore him, but he said, 'No, I'd like to see it. I've never had a family tree until now; it was just me and Jordan.'

'I'd never thought about it like that,' said Debbie. Jonathan explained that when Jordan was born, it felt as if there was finally 'another one of me' around — and now, suddenly, there were all these people in his life. 'My aunties, uncles — everybody's spoken to or written to him.'

The hardest bit of the journey was, of course, coming home, but Debbie held on to one thing: 'I feel so lucky.'

Almost as soon as they returned, the next trips were being planned. Ben, his partner and their daughter, together with Debbie's mum and stepdad, were due to visit Jonathan in the autumn of 2011. They were planning to go to Las Vegas too, and to take a road trip. When Ben and his partner get married in summer 2012, Jonathan, Rachel and Jordan are coming over for the wedding. After the visit to Corfe Castle and Stonehenge, they'd said they wanted to travel elsewhere in Europe, for the experience — Brian suggested Wales, but no one took him up on that, and they're hoping to make a short trip to France instead.

Jonathan was due to come over for Christmas 2011 too. He was to spend Christmas Day with Debbie and Brian, and then Boxing Day with his brothers, their partners and their children. Debbie was planning to make it a special trip; her daughter-in-law Sarah suggested she prepare twenty-seven stockings for all those years Jonathan missed out on.

It hasn't taken long for Jonathan to fit in with his brothers, and they're all very close already. They all tease Debbie, and Jonathan now joins in — a sure sign that not only is he comfortable with them, but so much like them too. 'We were just about to have a photograph taken, and he said to me, 'You've got . . . ' and he indicated that I had something on my front teeth. 'Oh no! Where?' and he smiled and laughed, 'Only kidding.' He takes the mickey out of my accent, and the way I talk. He says, 'You sound like somebody from the deep south,' and then launches into a Forrest Gump accent.

'He is so loved, and he has been so loved all these years — he's always been part of our lives. I'm so happy now that I can talk to people about him: 'Oh, my son's coming over, I spoke to my son yesterday.' It's changed my life immensely. There was this huge gap that I never thought I'd be able to fill. It helps if you've got other children to concentrate on, but he's somebody in his own right. Nobody can replace him.'

5

Jeannie, Hoping to Find Her Brother

'I don't remember Geoffrey going out of the door. I don't know if I kissed him goodbye even. I do remember that I cried, for a very long time when I went to bed. I wanted him back.'

Jeannie Elgar was born in Surrey during World War Two, in 1942. Her mother lived in Pimlico, in the centre of London, so, as with many children from the city, she was sent to live in the country, far from the bombs, and later the missiles, that fell on the capital. Jeannie went to live with her grandparents in Wales. Jeannie's uncles had all joined up and were fighting in the war, including her uncle John, who had lied about his age so that he could serve in the navy. He was torpedoed more than once when his ship was crossing the North Atlantic, and was lucky to survive. When there was thunder in the air, Jeannie would crawl under the kitchen table, doing what everyone in London had been told to do in the event of a bomb raid — her mother was bombed out of her home twice.

In the aftermath of the war, a lot of families struggled financially, and Jeannie's was no different — except that, unusually, her mother brought her and her younger brother Geoffrey up on her own. Geoffrey was four years younger than Jeannie, and all three lived in a small two-room flat in Glamorgan Street in Pimlico. The two children shared the same father, but he wasn't part of their lives at all, and their mother was left to look after them, and to work to keep them. 'She was under a lot of stress because she was working and there was no father providing for us, no extra money coming in. There wasn't the financial help that there is nowadays for parents, and she found the financial strain too much.' Jeannie's mother was strict with her children, and Jeannie liked it when her grandmother travelled up from Wales to visit them. 'I loved my grandmother. She would send me a half-crown postal order at Christmas and on birthdays — she was very good like that.'

In the March before she was eighteen, Jeannie went to stay with her grandmother in Wales for a week. While she was there, her grandmother took her to one side. 'I don't know why nobody's told you,' she said to Jeannie — and she went on to say that Jeannie's 'uncle' John was in fact her brother.

John, born in 1926, was sixteen years older than Jeannie, and had been brought up by his grandparents. By the time Jeannie knew he was her brother, he was married with six children. 'He was very nice, and we got on very well, but I didn't see a lot of him, because he lived in Wales. He gave me away when I got married.'

By then Jeannie lived with just her mother. When she was eight and Geoffrey four, Geoffrey was adopted.

Jeannie doesn't have any very specific memories of playing with Geoffrey, but she clearly remembers their relationship being like that of most brothers and sisters. 'Obviously I loved him, but we did fight, as brother and sisters always do, I think — as my own children and grandchildren used to do.' But she is also certain that the two of them were very close. 'I remember us playing together in Wales, where my grandmother lived. I remember reading to him, because obviously I was older, and we played with toys, although we didn't have a lot. We played the sort of games that children did, with balls and running about and that kind of thing. I was very bossy — that's probably in my nature — and because of the age gap of nearly four years, I think I probably did boss my little brother about quite a bit.'

She doesn't have a strong memory of him as a baby, and she wonders where he was in those early days, as she feels sure she would recall having a baby in the house to look after. 'I wonder if he wasn't with us at that time, because it's quite strange not to have memories of him as a baby.' She does, however, have a strong image of him as a small child. 'Geoffrey was a lovely-looking boy. He had fair, curly hair and blue eyes. He was very angelic looking — which I don't think he was all the time. From what I remember, he was quite funny and very loving — and I loved him.' Thanks to his angelic looks, Geoffrey drew a lot of attention from people.

'I think he was mischievous, but I think he was also rather a sensitive boy, so although he liked to run and jump, like all little boys do, I don't think he was a particularly aggressive personality at all.'

In the summer of 1950 Geoffrey went away with a couple on holiday to Scotland. The wife, Bunty, was the daughter of the doctor who, at the time, Jeannie's mother worked for. In later life, Jeannie discovered that Bunty had been unable to have children and she thinks the trip was an attempt to see if Geoffrey could become their child. All she ever knew about the holiday was a photograph she saw of Geoffrey on top of a hayrick.

For whatever reason, Geoffrey came back from the holiday, but some time later, Jeannie was at home when there was a knock at the door, and a couple, both dressed in suits, came in. Her mother introduced them: Mr and Mrs Smith. They had come to take her brother away to adopt him.

'I didn't know who Mr and Mrs Smith were. My mother introduced them to me, and then there was quite a lot of conversation and I was nervous. I thought they were some kind of officials, for some reason, possibly because they were in suits. They seemed quite nice.'

'I can still see the couple in my mind's eye. We only had two rooms in the house, and I remember sitting on the arm of the chair in the little sitting room with my mother and Mr and Mrs Smith on the other side of the fireplace. I seem to remember Mrs Smith asking me if I would ever leave my mother, and I shrank back and said that no, I wouldn't. I really don't know what I was thinking at the time. I know now that they'd come to take Geoffrey, and I think I thought that they might take me as well.'

Whether Mrs Smith thought that the two children would be happier together, or whether she'd taken a look around the place and believed that Jeannie would be better off with them is something Jeannie doesn't know. What did happen, though, is that Geoffrey left with them. 'I don't remember exactly Geoffrey going out of the door. I don't know if I kissed him goodbye even, so that's very sad.' Even after all these years, it was still too sad a memory for Jeannie to look back on. She wasn't sure if she even realised that he was going away, never to come back; he might have been going on another holiday, for all she knew. And of course, as she was very young, she did have mixed feelings: 'I was only eight when Geoffrey left and, to be honest, I was probably a little bit jealous because I felt he was the blond, blue-eyed favourite of the family.'

At what point later that day Jeannie started missing Geoffrey, she's not sure. 'When I went to bed that night I cried for a very long time. I sensed that something was very wrong, because I was so upset and I was crying so much. I wanted him back, as I knew somehow that he had gone for good. I don't know how I knew; I just felt so sad. I hadn't cried when he'd been taken away on holiday to Scotland — at least I don't remember doing so — but now I wanted to get up and say to my mother, 'I want him back,' but I was too afraid to do that. I felt lonely and on my own. I did love him.'

Like so many children in a similar situation, Jeannie felt that somehow Geoffrey not being there anymore was her fault. 'I felt guilty because I should've saved him. I should've kept him at home and said to my mother that I would be a very, very good girl if she let him stay with us. But I didn't do that, and I'm so sorry that I didn't do that. I do feel guilty because I feel that I didn't behave as a big sister should. I should've somehow stopped Geoffrey from leaving.'

Over the next few months, Jeannie learned that 'Mr and Mrs Smith' — she never believed those were their real names — had taken him to Australia and on to Fiji. Now she was alone at home with her mother.

'I think things were different at the time when Geoffrey was adopted. It was harder for a single mother to look after the two of us, and she was working and obviously very stressed. I'm sure she felt that it would be a good life for him, better than the one that he would have had in this country. I know that I couldn't have done that — once I'd had my children, I couldn't bear to think of parting with any of them. I think it probably took a lot of courage on my mother's part to do that.'

Jeannie never really got on with her mother, who had a quick temper. She was violent towards Jeannie and intimidated her. She used to say to Jeannie that she wanted to have her adopted, but nobody would take her. 'I was older than Geoffrey, and people want to adopt younger children, I guess. When we had rows, when I was in trouble, my mother would often say, 'I'm going to put you in a home.'' Jeannie would believe her, and would spend anxious moments looking out of a window, waiting for someone to come and take her away. She used this threat regularly, along with violence.

Jeannie's mother was obviously a very bitter person, and from what Jeannie has been able to piece together in later life, probably very disappointed with her lot. 'She always used to tell me about her glamorous life when she was younger. She was very pretty as a young woman.' She told Jeannie that when she was in her twenties she had danced with the Prince of Wales, when he came to Cardiff, long before he became the Duke of Windsor. During the war, she worked for the Ministry of Defence, but Jeannie is not sure what role she had — 'clerking, I suppose'. Her mother was very intelligent, very good at maths, and she played the violin when she was young. She was also very independent, and a very hard worker. For her to end up in a two-room flat in Pimlico must have seemed like a come-down.

There are things about her mother that Jeannie admires. 'She brought me up well, to have a sense of pride, to read books and appreciate things.' However, her mother was also very cruel to her, harping on about her own attractiveness as a young woman and comparing Jeannie unfavourably to herself. 'I always used to think I wouldn't be as pretty as she had been, and I always had a bit of an inferiority complex. When I was older, I was still scared of my mother, because she could be very sarcastic and hurtful. To this day, I can't take anybody being like that. It just makes me shrivel up inside.'

Her mother worked in a variety of jobs during Jeannie's childhood and teenage years. When she was older, Jeannie would accompany her when she was working as a home help. It was only when she had grown up that Jeannie was able to look back, put two and two together and see that it was as a result of the kind of work her mother did that her brother Geoffrey had been adopted.

Her mother had worked for a local doctor in Pimlico, and it was his daughter, Bunty, who had taken Geoffrey away on holiday. For whatever reason, Geoffrey had not stayed with her and her husband, but Jeannie believes it was through this doctor's surgery that her mother had been introduced to Mr and Mrs Smith. Jeannie has no solid information about this though, because her mother destroyed any documents relating to Geoffrey before she died, including the photograph Jeannie remembers seeing of Geoffrey on top of a hayrick. The only photographs she had left of him were of him as a small boy, and one of the two of them together, with Geoffrey holding her hand.

One aspect of Jeannie's mother's personality, that she was always anti-men, is perhaps a little easier to get to the bottom of. Jeannie's father, Arthur Leonard Davison, was 'quite a Casanova'. He had joined the army when young, although, unlike his father, who had joined the Royal Garrison Artillery and worked his way up the ranks during World War One (being awarded a medal on the way) to the post of Second Lieutenant, her father went into the Grenadier Guards.

Initially her father had served abroad, in Egypt, but he had left the army in the mid 1930s. He went on to the reserve list, so when war broke out, he went back into the Grenadier Guards. He was taken off the beaches at Dunkirk when the British Expeditionary Force had to leave France, but apart from that, Jeannie doesn't know much more about his military career.

What she does know is that he was married, and not to her mother. She also knows that the girl he married was pregnant, and that she might have a half-sister somewhere in the UK. 'I've tried to find her, but it's really difficult, because my mother was the Other Woman. They had a child, a girl, and his wife had a second girl but she was adopted and my father is not named on the birth certificate.' Jeannie wonders, of course, if there are others: 'I think he did have a string; he was quite prolific.'

* * *

Although Geoffrey was gone, Jeannie and her mother did have one piece of news. A letter arrived — Jeannie doesn't know exactly when — which her mother read out. Mr and Mrs Smith were on the HMS *Orion*, bound for Australia and then the island of Fiji, and they wrote with some news about Geoffrey. 'I don't remember what the letter said, except they indicated that Geoffrey was fine during the day, but at night he was calling for his Jeannie.' It was the last Jeannie heard of her brother for many years.

The details of the ship and its voyage meant nothing to the young Jeannie. 'It could've been on the moon, as far as I was concerned, especially growing up in the time that I did, when travel wasn't so common. It seemed another world, and I hardly knew where Fiji was.' One thing was certain to her, however, even though she didn't know how far away those places actually were: 'I knew it was too far away for me to ever see him again.'

Jeannie's mother never spoke about Geoffrey again. It was as if he had never existed. Such was her fear of her mother's temper, Jeannie never asked her anything about him. 'My mother was never very communicative, and I was afraid that if I spoke about Geoffrey, it would upset her and then she would get very angry with me. She indicated that she didn't want to talk about it, but many years later, she did tell me that the people that Geoffrey had gone on holiday to Scotland with had wanted to adopt him, but that had fallen through because they were a childless couple. I think she must've been thinking about having him adopted quite early on.' The significance of the phrase 'a childless couple' didn't mean anything to Jeannie then — it was only later on that those words made sense to her.

Meanwhile she grew up, but she never forgot about her younger brother, and she spoke to her friends about him. 'When I was at secondary school, I was at home with one of my school friends, and we were talking about Geoffrey. I told her about the letter and, very naughtily, I went and searched through my mother's possessions, and I found the letter. We read it, and then I put it back again.'

Before she was married, when she was twenty-one, Jeannie decided she would try to trace her missing relatives. The laws regarding adoption were strict — and Jeannie still believed Mr and Mrs Smith were not the couple's real names. Still, she spoke to the Salvation Army, who were able to track down her father, even if they could do nothing to help her find Geoffrey. Jeannie met her father, who came up from his home in Swansea for the day to see her, and that was the only time she saw him. Even now, she only has one photograph of him in her possession. 'I started looking for Geoffrey with the Salvation Army. I thought they would be able to trace him for me. They weren't able to do so, but they didn't give me a reason why. I just heard back from them that they weren't able to help me.'

Jeannie mistakenly left the letter she'd received from the Salvation Army regarding her search lying around, and her mother found it and demanded to know what Jeannie was doing. Her mother's power over her was still strong. 'I lied, and I think she knew it.'

Over the next fifteen years, increasingly dismayed by her lack of success in tracing Geoffrey's whereabouts, Jeannie wondered if he even remembered her, and after a while began to doubt she would ever see him again. 'I couldn't search thoroughly while my mother was alive. I was too afraid of what she would say.'

When her mother died, in 1982, Jeannie went through her effects to see if she could find the letter and the photograph she remembered to aid her in her search. She found nothing, not a sign of the treasure she'd been seeking. 'My mother destroyed the letter before she died.' It wasn't just the letter she'd thrown away; everything to do with Geoffrey had gone. In the end, the only things Jeannie had to remind her of her brother were the things given to her by her grandmother.

By now Jeannie was happily married, with a family of her own. She named her youngest son Jeffrey. As a reaction, perhaps, to her own fractured life, and recalling also the efforts of her own grandmother, Jeannie has remained involved in her family's life, through to the grandchildren she has now.

The obstacles in the way of her search for her brother seemed to mount up. Not only did she think the name of his adoptive parents was false, she had no idea of where in the world they had taken Geoffrey. Maybe the family had moved on from Australia and Fiji. Where could she look then? The secrecy that surrounded adoption in those days prevented an easy solution. Also, none of the systems in place to help people search after adoption seemed geared to help her; they were mostly for people searching for their birth parents, or vice versa, and no one seemed to be set up to search for a missing sibling.

Jeannie never stopped searching for Geoffrey, and tried every route she could think of. 'I tried the Passport Office because I thought there must be some sort of record. Maybe Mr and Mrs Smith had to get him a passport of his own to go abroad. I tried the General Register Office, where they've got lists of adoptions, but that's very difficult unless you know what name they went by when they were adopted. At that time, I still thought that Mr and Mrs Smith were assumed names. I also looked at various databases, and I joined Genes Reunited and put his name on the web to try and find him. I pursued my family history again, trying to find out anything I could that would help me find my brother.'

'I tried NORCAP, and then I tried the Child Migrants Trust, because I was afraid that he might've been sent to Australia and abandoned, as so many children were. I tried the General Records Office.' But then Jeannie made one of her breakthroughs. 'I'd heard that you could look up records for the primary school in Westminster that we both went to. I found the piece of paper that told you where the children from the nursery had gone (because some children had moved away, or for some other reason hadn't gone up into the Infants), and I found my own entry. Then I found Geoffrey's, and it just said 'Fiji'. That's all. It didn't say 'adopted', just 'Fiji'. It was very odd to see it in black and white, somehow, to know that he had gone. But it was confirmation of what my mother had said, so it was good in that way.'

Her second great breakthrough came when she was able to obtain the passenger records of the ship that Geoffrey had left the UK on. The passenger records from HMS *Orion*, dated 1950, showed that a Mr Smith had travelled with his wife; he was forty-one and his wife was forty-four. He was listed as a civil servant, travelling to Fiji via Australia. With them were two boys: four-year-old Geoffrey and a baby boy, only six months old, listed as Master R. Welch.

Fired up with the excitement of this find, Jeannie set out to discover who the other boy was, thinking that if she could locate his relatives, maybe she would find that they were searching for him — and that they might make more headway in looking for the two boys if they combined their resources.

'Because Geoffrey had been born in Lambeth Hospital, I thought Mr and Mrs Smith might well have found 'Master Welch' there too. I went through the GRO and I picked out an R. Welch — Richard — who'd been born in Lambeth Hospital, and sent away for a copy of his birth certificate.' Sadly, though, Jeannie's hunch was wrong: Richard Welch was too young, by three months, to be the 'R. Welch' in the passenger list.

The next thing Jeannie thought to try were the embarkation lists, both from the UK and Australia. Again, she drew a blank. 'I thought that this was it, that I would be able to progress from here. But I couldn't find anything on the Australian websites, so that wasn't any good.'

Becoming more desperate, Jeannie turned to Social Services ('I thought maybe they had arranged the adoption, but they weren't able to help me') and she even thought of contacting the Fijian government, through its embassy in London. 'The records for Fiji are, as far as I could gather, non-existent, so I wasn't hopeful.'

Jeannie then went back to scour all of the evidence she had gathered up till then, in case it yielded up a clue that she had overlooked before. 'The records showed that the adopted father was a civil servant, but was he an English civil servant, or was he an Australian who was posted to Fiji? Maybe they were in the diplomatic service or something like that?' After years of looking for a Geoffrey Davison, she now went back over old ground, looking for a Geoffrey Smith — but 'it's not the easiest surname in the world to research'. At least now she knew that Mr and Mrs Smith were their real names, so any doubts she'd had over the years about them were put to rest.

At this point Jeannie came across the *Long Lost Family* team, and asked them to help her in her search for Geoffrey. At the time, she told them: 'I'm constantly on the internet trying to find him. I think I've tried everything, and I really think I've come to a brick wall now. I don't know what else to do, and time is really of the essence. It gets harder as you get older, because you don't know how much time you've got left. I want my family to meet Geoffrey, to know him; my husband has never seen him, and he's just a name to my children and grandchildren as well.

'I imagine him to be tall. I still see the fair hair, but I suppose now it must be grey. I imagine that if he's lived in Australia, he's done a lot of sport, that he's tanned, an outdoors type. Perhaps he took after his adopted father and went into the Civil Service. I imagine all sorts of things. It's a worry because I don't know if he's had a happy life. I so want him to have had that. A happy life, and for the adoption to have been a good thing for him.'

Jeannie feels that she has been lucky in her life, with her marriage and her children and grandchildren, and she would love to know that Geoffrey has had the same things. 'I'd love it if he had married and had children, and perhaps even grandchildren, like me. Perhaps he's not in Australia; perhaps he's living in this country. That would be fantastic. That would be the very, very best thing.'

'Sixty years have gone by since he went, and he could be anywhere. He could be in the next street and I wouldn't know. I don't know what he looks like. I don't know what else to do. Does he even remember me? He may not even know that he was adopted, because in those days people didn't tell you these things. For him to know he has a sister who's missed him would be good.

'The one thing I would like to know about Geoffrey is whether he had a good life. Is he or was he happy? That's paramount, I think. My very worst fear is that I will never find him, and never know what happened to him.'

The *Long Lost Family* team took over the search, using the vital pieces of evidence that Jeannie had unearthed. As we've seen, the only trace that Jeannie could find of Geoffrey showed that in 1950 he was on board a ship bound for Fiji via Australia. However, the Fijian and Australian records of the time showed there was no sign of the Smith family disembarking. Undeterred, they went back to Mr Smith's entry on the passenger list, and decided to follow up on his occupation. If he had worked for the Civil Service, it was a good bet that it was for the Foreign Office. The Foreign Office was able to confirm that an Arthur Smith had been posted to Fiji as a customs controller. Unfortunately that was the last record of Arthur Smith in the Foreign Office Archive. The team could only assume that he had changed jobs or retired, so now they needed to make an educated guess as to where Arthur and his family had ended up. According to Foreign Office records, Arthur Smith had gone to school in Bermuda, so maybe that's where the couple had taken

Geoffrey and their other adopted son?

A search in Bermuda turned up no record of an Arthur Smith, but they did find a book published locally, *Senior Citizens' Biographies*, which contained a chapter about an Edith Irene Smith, who had lived on the island. Crucially, the biography confirmed that she had previously lived in Fiji with her husband, who had worked for the Foreign Office. The researchers placed an advert in the main Bermuda newspaper, the *Royal Gazette*, asking if anyone knew anything more about the Smith family. Lots of people remembered her, but no one had any contact details for Geoffrey. Then they took a call from a woman who said her father, Robert, was Mr and Mrs Smith's son, and that he had had an adopted brother called Geoffrey. Robert was clearly the 'Master R. Welch' of the ship's records, the one Jeannie had thought might be Richard, and the reason she'd found no trace of his birth in Lambeth was because Robert was born in Cardiff, where HMS *Orion* had sailed from.

Nicky Campbell travelled to Bermuda to meet Robert. Sadly the first thing Robert told him was that Geoffrey had died in 1979, in a powerboat-racing accident. He was only thirty-four years old at the time. Did he, wondered Nicky, ever talk about his sister

Jeannie? 'He spoke about her all the time,' said Robert. 'He told me he had a sister that was four years older than him, and he used to go looking for her because he had a mental picture of her in his mind, and he swore he would recognise her if he saw her. And if you know you have a sister out there, even if you have a wonderful family who have taken care of all your needs and everything, you still have that desire to go and find your biological sister.'

Robert was keen to stress to Nicky how happy Geoffrey's life had been. After Geoffrey had left his mother and sister in London, he'd been adopted by one of the wealthiest families in Bermuda. He was educated at an exclusive boarding school in England, and went on to become a record producer in the 1970s. Robert showed Nicky some photographs of Geoffrey — one of them must have been taken very soon after Geoffrey was adopted by the Smiths. Nicky noticed that Geoffrey held his father's hand in the same way he held Jeannie's hand in the photograph she had of him. 'He had a good life — a wonderful life,' said Robert, who became tearful at the memory of his long-dead brother. 'Now she can put the questions aside and be happy for him.' And he added, 'I can't wait to meet Jeannie.'

It was now the sad task of the *Long Lost Family* team to tell Jeannie that although they'd traced Geoffrey, he was dead. 'I couldn't believe it — he could only have been thirty-three.' Jeannie wondered what she had been doing in 1979, when Geoffrey had died. And she tried hard to remember where she had been, and what she'd been doing, the day he'd actually died. She couldn't help but think also of all the efforts she'd made over the years. 'I spent all that time looking for him. I had no idea that he was dead. All that effort, and he wasn't around anymore.'

After Jeannie had had some days to absorb the heartbreaking news, Davina met up with her to show her the photographs that Robert had sent them. Jeannie was of course subdued and studied them all carefully. 'He's still got his curly hair and a gap in his teeth — my mother had that.' Seeing the photographs of Geoffrey with his adoptive parents, and hearing from Davina what Robert had said about their lives together, Jeannie was at least comforted to know that the adoption had been successful and that Geoffrey had been happy. 'It means the world, to know that he had good parents,' she told Davina. And of course the thought that Geoffrey had indeed never forgotten her —

that he had talked about her to Robert — meant so much to her.

Davina also had a letter from Robert to pass on.

> Dear Jeannie,
>
> I hope that this letter finds you well. Geoff had such a vivid memory of you. He always said to me, 'I will know her when I see her.' Geoff spoke of you often, and I also felt my sister was missing. I would love to meet you. I have so many stories to tell you. You are always welcome in my home. I look forward to meeting you soon.
>
> Sincerely, Robert.

The letter touched Jeannie, and Robert's evident wish to ensure that Jeannie learnt as much as he could tell her about Geoffrey moved her to tears. 'I would like him to be my brother, because he was so close to Geoffrey — an adopted brother would be nice.'

After meeting Jeannie, Davina said, 'That was very traumatic for Jeannie, but the realisation that Geoffrey had never forgotten her, had even searched for her, as she'd been searching for him, along with the fact that she'll be going to Bermuda to meet Robert and learn all about Geoffrey and say goodbye

— all of those things may finally give her some kind of closure.'

The reunion

A month later, Jeannie flew to Bermuda. Robert was very much looking forward to meeting her, as 'In my mind, she always has been my sister. It's just that I'd never seen her. This is wonderful.'

When Robert came to meet her at her hotel, Jeannie couldn't help but jump up and rush to greet him, so moved was she to finally meet someone who'd known Geoffrey as an adult. Robert called her 'my little big sister', and said that she reminded him of Geoffrey: 'The smile is the same.' Jeannie wanted to know what their childhood had been like, and Robert said, 'We were regular kids growing up. We had a wonderful time. You couldn't ask for better parents to be adopted by. They were super parents. He had a good life, a really, really good life. He spent quite a lot of time looking for you.'

Jeannie told Robert of her fear that she had been forgotten. 'I was always worried that he would not remember me at all.' However, Robert was able to reassure her of this: 'He was telling me about you when I was four years old. He remembered you — there wasn't a year that went by when he didn't talk about you. He used to look for you in Cardiff — I don't know why. He would go on little pub crawls, and would approach people, chat them up, ask them. I would always encourage him, because as far as I was concerned, his sister was my sister. He had to find you.'

Jeannie was delighted to hear this: 'And now you've got me.'

Robert reiterated that Geoffrey did think about her a lot as they made their way over to the cemetery where Geoffrey is buried. Jeannie laid some flowers on his grave, and after she had gathered herself together, she summed up: 'I feel I've maybe lost Geoffrey, but I have gained another brother in Robert. He's been so kind to talk about Geoffrey, and now I know that Geoffrey had never forgotten me.'

After the programme

For Jeannie, the time after filming had finished and before the programme was broadcast was just as busy for her in terms of her research as before. She had learned some extraordinary things while she was in Bermuda, and when she returned to England she was able to look into them herself.

The first was that Geoffrey had been married, to Julie, and had had a son, Richard. He and Julie had separated, and although Julie was now living in Australia, she contacted Jeannie to tell her more about Geoffrey's life. She too had always known about Jeannie, and she told her that Geoffrey had made many efforts to try to find her — she understood that he'd even argued with his adoptive parents about this. Maybe they let slip that she had a Welsh background — and that might explain why he went looking for Jeannie in Cardiff. They apparently told him that his biological mother had been ill and couldn't manage two children.

Julie was able to tell Jeannie all sorts of things about Geoffrey — when he'd come back to the UK to go to school, for example. She said she had a photograph of him coming first in a pole-vaulting competition. She also told Jeannie what Geoffrey remembered of his life in London with Jeannie — he recalled playing hide and seek, and that he used to hide in a cupboard. Julie's brother, who lived here in the UK, was watching television the night the programme was broadcast and — on seeing Geoffrey — rang ITV to ask them to pass his details on to Jeannie.

Geoffrey's son Richard also lived in the

UK, and Jeannie met him. She was so sorry that she hadn't known about him when he was younger, because she would have liked to have been a proper aunt to him — to have bought him presents and, most importantly, to have helped him through the awful days after his father's accident. For his part, he was disappointed that no one had told him about Jeannie earlier; not that anyone knew how to find her, but he would have liked to have known she was there, somewhere.

Jeannie was then contacted by Anne, Geoffrey's girlfriend at the time of his death, and the two of them had lunch when she came over from Bermuda. Anne too knew about Jeannie from Geoffrey. Jeannie also heard from Margaret, a girlfriend of Geoffrey's way back in the early 1970s, who wrote to her about Geoffrey, saying that he was very sweet, shy and kind.

Jeannie continued to look for anything she could find on the internet, as she sought to complete her family tree. She found lots of relatives on her mother's side. One day, out of idle curiosity, she entered her mother and father's names and the dates she knew about on a register. Along with some of the expected results, another name popped out: Arthur Leonard (Jeannie's father's first names), with an address in Surrey as his place of birth. His date of birth was midway between hers and Geoffrey's. Jeannie knew she had been born in Surrey, but she regarded this find as merely an odd coincidence, and thought no more about it. 'I wrote the index number down, but didn't do anything.'

A couple of months later she had discovered two people whom she thought might turn out to be her father's siblings and, to confirm this, wrote off for their birth certificates. On a whim, she added in the index number of Arthur Leonard's birth certificate. 'I thought, 'It's £10, why not. I'll get all three.'' The first one she received back was Arthur Leonard's, and to her amazement it listed her parents as the child's parents. There could be no doubt about it: 'My mother's name, Aileen, was quite unusual in those days; the father was down as serving in the Grenadier Guards, which mine was during the war; the address was Glamorgan Street in Pimlico — and we lived in three houses in that street.' Jeannie remembered living in two of those houses — number twenty-eight and number ninety-one — but this listed one she didn't recall: number one.

She had unearthed a brother she knew nothing about, born when she was two and given up for adoption right away. 'Adopted' was written on the birth certificate, so Arthur Leonard would have gone straight from the nursing home to his new family.

Using the services of an Adoption Support Agency, the only route in making contact with someone who is adopted, Jeannie was able to make contact with her younger brother. The agency found out her brother's adopted name — something inaccessible to anyone else — and then traced him. An intermediary made contact with him before putting him in touch with Jeannie. She learned that, after he was adopted, his parents had changed his name — to, amazingly enough, John (also the name of Jeannie's older brother). 'I wondered whether he would want to know. I think he was a bit wary. My mother and father weren't married, and I think he thought I might not be a very respectable person. I was careful to put in the letter that I'd been married for forty-odd years and had three children, all of them married, and that I'd worked for the Camden Local Education Authority.'

He did write back, and after an exchange of letters he suggested the two of them meet. 'I met him and his wife. He was very nice. He had some photos of his family, and I had photos of his mum and dad and his grandmother and grandfather.' Jeannie also gave him copies of the family trees that she is still compiling. She wanted to see photographs of him when he was a small boy, to see if he looked like the Geoffrey she remembered. 'I did say, 'Can you show me a photo of you when you were younger?' He found some in the attic: he was blond and curly-haired, like Geoffrey and my older brother John.' Of course Geoffrey had changed over the years, and before he died, in the photographs Robert had shown her, 'He had this funny sort of Afro-Caribbean hairstyle that people had in the 1970s, especially in the music business.' She found it difficult to visualise the young Geoffrey in the man in front of her.

John told Jeannie that he was told about his adoption when he was twenty-one, but he had guessed before then. He also said that his mother had told him that his biological mother had given up her child because she already had two others, and that she couldn't manage another one. She had added that the father didn't want any more children either, something Jeannie acknowledges is very likely.

He has since said to Jeannie that his youngest son particularly wanted to meet her, and that his granddaughter had seen the programme and also wanted to meet 'that lady'. John was due to give a talk to his local club on 'Who Am I?' He invited Jeannie along to the talk, which she was thrilled about.

Part of John's early story fascinated Jeannie because it enabled her to piece together what she thinks was the case regarding Geoffrey's adoption too. When the programme uncovered Mr and Mrs Smith's history, Jeannie learned that Mrs Smith had been a nurse. With the money they had, Jeannie assumes that the adoption was a private one, and that it was arranged through the doctor that her mother had worked for. John told Jeannie that his adoption had gone through the local doctor in Pimlico. It turned out that he was brought up down the road from Jeannie, in a flat overlooking the river in Dolphin Square, until he was twelve. When Jeannie was fourteen and went to Buckingham Gate School, the schoolgirls would go past Dolphin Square and gaze at the swimming pool, 'to see how the other people lived'.

Even though Jeannie's hope — that she would be reunited with her brother after sixty years apart — proved to be fruitless, she nevertheless was very happy that she had taken part in the programme. She has met people who, while fascinated by her story, have said to her that they didn't think they could go through the process she'd gone through, that they couldn't put themselves through such an emotional wringer. Jeannie always replies, 'But you would if it was the last chance available to you. If nothing else was going to work — if you'd tried everything you could think of — then of course you'd turn to an organisation with resources and contacts, and you'd grab this chance, especially if you thought this might be your last opportunity to learn the truth.'

As Jeannie said, 'If it hadn't been for the programme, I wouldn't know he was dead, and I wouldn't know he remembered me and tried to find me. That was a comfort.'

She was never even sure that they would ever find him, as she thought she'd tried every possible route. 'Originally I thought that they'd come back and say they couldn't find him. I wasn't even sure that they'd find him when they were filming. Or I thought that maybe they would, but he'd tell them he didn't want to know.' It is thanks to the efforts and expertise of the programme-makers that they eventually uncovered the truth for her.

Jeannie goes back to her photographs of Geoffrey often. The little boy in the early pictures is the one she remembers, of course. She's not sure that he really is holding hands with his father in the same way that he held hands with her, and she thinks he looks lost. 'He'd only been with them perhaps a few days — who knows when that was taken.' But in the later photographs, Geoffrey is happy and smiling.

Nothing will make up for what Jeannie feels she lost, but she is glad the *Long Lost Family* team got the result they did. 'I'm really grateful. I'm lucky they took up my search. I'd always advise people to go for it.'

She has been approached by people who want to tell her about their experiences and about the people they would like to be reunited with. Once, when she was out shopping with her daughter Jenny, a woman approached her outside Bond Street tube and told her about her brother who'd disappeared when he was twenty-one. She never knew what had happened to him, twenty-odd years ago. At least for Jeannie, that uncertainty is a thing of the past.

6

Kirsty, Trying to Trace Her Son

'It doesn't matter what you think you're ready for; the reality is very different. You might think you've got complete control, but when you meet that person, that's gone. Just be prepared for anything really. You just don't know what you're going to come up with.'

Kirsty West had a normal childhood, but things changed for her when she was a teenager. On a summer holiday, at the age of fifteen, she met a boy, and they had a relationship. At the end of the holiday, they both returned to the UK. Their relationship continued for a time, but eventually came to an end. A short while later, Kirsty discovered she was pregnant. Horrified, she chose to ignore the pregnancy, hoping it would go away. She didn't tell the child's father, nor her own mother and father. 'I was terrified about being pregnant, really terrified. I didn't want to talk about it to anybody.' She tried to carry on with her life as normal and put her pregnancy out of her mind. However, 'After a couple of months I knew something was going on. The first time I accepted it was really happening was the first time I felt it move.'

She spoke to a few very close friends about what was happening, but she managed to conceal what was going on so well that even they weren't completely sure she was pregnant. One of these friends would later become her partner, Andy. He said, 'I don't know whether I was supposed to know or not, but I did know, although I didn't believe it, because there weren't any physical signs. You wouldn't have known she was pregnant.' One of the toughest things for Kirsty to get through was a family wedding. Kirsty, a bridesmaid, was beautifully dressed in a specially made outfit. 'My pregnancy caused some issues when it was being fitted, as I was growing. My sister thought I was just getting fat.' It took a huge effort from her to avoid any questions about her weight. 'Nobody knew. I'd got so used to holding it in. I was sucking my stomach in tightly.'

* * *

Keeping things secret from her family and most of her friends was hard enough, but somehow Kirsty managed to convince even herself that the pregnancy was only a figment of her imagination. 'Although I'd stand there, look at myself in the mirror, feel all the kicks and everything, I kept saying to myself, 'It's okay, it'll go away. Don't worry about it.' I really convinced myself.' Looking back, Kirsty finds it hard to make sense of what was going on in her mind. 'It was really stupid. I can't understand, in my adult head, why I did that. I was in complete denial. I was young, I was frightened — fear had quite a lot to do with it.'

Eventually, of course, this could go on no longer. When Kirsty was nine months pregnant, the inevitable happened. 'About teatime, I felt a bit strange, so I went up to use the bathroom, and my waters broke. I just paced around all night, in my room, trying to get into a position where I wasn't in so much pain. It was a very, very long, lonely night. On my own, scared stiff, not knowing what to do.'

The following morning, her mother rang the doctor's surgery, and he came out to visit the sixteen-year-old girl. 'The doctor confirmed to my mum what was happening. Of course she immediately started crying. 'Why didn't you tell me? Didn't you feel you could trust me?' It was a very traumatic time for everybody.'

The family were all very distressed by what had happened, and understandably her father and mother's initial reaction was anger. (Kirsty found out years later that while she was in hospital, her father went to see a solicitor, to see if they could track down the baby's father and prosecute him, as Kirsty was only just sixteen.) But with their daughter also deeply shocked and only just coping after her harrowing experience, they rapidly calmed down and agreed to support Kirsty in whatever decision she made.

Everything moved at such a rush for Kirsty, and as she had spent most of her pregnancy in denial, she didn't have any idea about what she really wanted for herself and her baby. She did know that she was very young and had nothing to offer a child, and that without a father around things would be tougher still for her and the baby. She realised that her baby would be better off with people who were ready to have a child. So while she was in hospital, she decided not to even look at her baby boy, and to give him up for adoption.

'I made the actual decision to have him adopted when I was giving birth to him. I said to the nurses, 'Don't let me see him; I'm not keeping him.' As they wheeled him out of the room, I caught a glimpse of him — all I saw was the top of his head. I felt that natural pull of 'he's my baby', but I was doing what was right for him and not thinking about what was right for me. I believed I was doing the right thing for him.'

The next couple of days were very tough for her. She lay on her hospital bed and wouldn't allow herself to go and see her son, whom she named Stephen. Her visitors were refused permission to see him too, as the nurses had decided that if Kirsty wasn't going to allow herself to see him, nobody else should be allowed to either. Kirsty had taken the harsh decision not to see her baby because she knew only too well how she had felt in those fleeting moments when she'd caught sight of the top of his head, and she realised that if she did succumb to the desire to go and see him, she would not be able to let him go — and the adoption would not take place. It was something she had to force herself to do, as the urge to keep him with her was very strong.

After she was discharged, her son remained in hospital for another few days before he was taken in by a foster family while the paperwork for the adoption went through. Kirsty found those days even harder: 'It was an awful, horrible time, those first few weeks, making decisions, signing bits of paper, all that stuff — it wasn't pleasant at all.' She put herself on autopilot, and drifted through the days, careful not to allow herself to think about her child, 'because I kept wanting to change my mind. I wanted to have him back.' At the time, all she had as a reminder of him was a Polaroid taken by one of the nurses in the hospital, just after he was born. He is sleeping, wrapped up tightly in a blanket, tufts of hair standing up.

Being back at home, and knowing her child was living in a village not far away from her family home was 'torturous'. This was the only time during those difficult days that Kirsty was grateful for being the age she was: 'It was probably a good thing that I couldn't drive because there were a few times when I think I would have ended up going up there. It was that difficult to stay away — it was hard.' As before, she kept her feelings to herself. No one knew just how desperately she felt the urge to keep her son with her.

Kirsty had been involved in the decision as to who would adopt her child. She was given two profiles by the social workers; each file detailed what the family was like and what they hoped to offer the child. There was never any doubt in Kirsty's mind that adoption, rather than placing him in care, was the right thing. 'I didn't want to see him go from pillar to post; that would have been horrible. I wanted him to have a proper family as soon as possible, to be settled somewhere.'

One of the prospective families had already adopted a little girl, and Kirsty thought they would be ideal for her son. Once the decision was made, she was shown a photograph of the three of them together, and was told the parents' first names. Within three weeks of her son's birth, his future was determined, although it would be many more weeks before all the court documents were signed and her son was officially adopted.

Finally the time came when the adoption process was completed and her baby was no longer with the foster family but settled for good. In some ways, this was a relief for Kirsty: 'Once he was in the adopted family's home, I knew I couldn't take him away. Knowing the adoption had gone through made it easier in a way because I knew I couldn't change my mind.' The day before he was placed with his new family, another photograph was taken, this time with the little curly-haired boy smiling as he lay on a rug. Kirsty kept both the photographs she had of her son carefully put away: 'I could get them out when I was on my own, and have a little cry. That's all I had to remember him by, my little man.'

Kirsty's family tried to support her through what they could see was a difficult time, but she found it hard to discuss her feelings with the people closest to her then. Instead, to start with, she did 'as a young person does, and went out and got drunk a lot, I blotted it out a bit . . . I put it away and buried it.' Gradually her family stopped talking about it, perhaps thinking that if Kirsty didn't want to open up, then not talking about it would help her. She had one friend who discussed things with her, but they didn't really talk about it that much, and Kirsty felt that everyone around her felt that what had happened had happened, and that was the end of it really — no one more so than herself, at least outwardly. However, the thought of her son was always there, and on special occasions — especially his birthday — she would take some time away from others to think about him, wondering what he was doing and how he was getting on. 'I didn't make an issue of it, but it was always there.'

Nearly ten years later, Kirsty and Andy got together, and have remained together since. Devastatingly for them both, they have been unable to have children, which only caused Kirsty more despair. 'I've tried not to let it show openly; inside is where all the pain's happening.' This led to her regretting even more her experiences at the age of sixteen, and once her son reached the age of eighteen, Kirsty decided she would start looking for him. She wondered what he knew about his adoption — and what he felt about it. She thought it was more likely than not that he'd been told, because he had an adopted sister, but what did it mean to him? Would he want to know more than that?

At first she wasn't sure how to go about looking, and started by reading material and watching programmes that had anything to do with adoption. She quickly discovered, though, that this wasn't going to be the best route for her, as she found herself ambushed by her emotions. 'I wasn't good at watching other people being reunited on television. I'd avoid that if I could; just seeing their joy was hard for me to watch.' She started searching on the internet. She would read about how the process of being reunited worked, how people felt both before and afterwards, what the pitfalls might be, how the adopted person felt about being found. And while she prepared herself as best she could this way, she also realised that the answers weren't always the same — that each situation varied, and each encounter was unique.

A new worry for her was when she realised that her son would be, as an adult, able to join the armed forces. She would wince every time a death of someone of the right age was announced in the wars abroad, and carefully checked the details when they were released. She felt no relief when she saw the photographs — that was still someone else's son.

When she walked the streets, she would stare at the faces of the boys passing her, hoping she might bump into him by chance. The need to know, the desire for information, was always there; she couldn't stop thinking about it.

A few years after her son was born, Kirsty started suffering from panic attacks. As she grew older, it became harder for her to leave the house, and she ended up almost agoraphobic, petrified about going anywhere. She was able to go on holiday, but only after a lot of effort on her part and under a lot of strain. She found travelling horrible, as being in crowds caused her to panic. To continue searching for her son, she resorted to placing adverts on bulletin boards, hoping he would read them.

Unfortunately she only knew the name she had given him at birth, and — by law — she was not allowed to know the name he had been given by his new family. That is why she was only allowed to know the first names of his parents. Therefore the only facts she could include in her plea were his date and place of birth — the hospital in Luton where he was born. She wrote:

> I was just sixteen then, and adoption seemed like the only choice, although later I am unsure that it really was and I have missed you every day. I would dearly love to find you and know what your life has been like up till now.
>
> Love always, forever hopeful that we may someday have contact, your birth mum Kirsty

The messages went unanswered.

But one of her messages was spotted by the *Long Lost Family* team, and she was invited to apply to them. She told the researchers that she was desperate to find her son, and although it was difficult to pursue the search while she found it hard to go outdoors, she could not put off her search for him any longer. She had spent years being scared that he would reject her, and was still not sure if it was the right thing to do, but she knew that she would not feel complete until her son knew that she wanted to have contact with him. She longed to know that he was okay, and it was her dream to be able to have a relationship with him.

Andy told the team, 'She needs to know

whether she did the right thing, and if that's all she finds out, if she was to be told, 'Yes, you did the right thing,' that would mean everything to her. It's like a dream for her, it's what she wants more than anything else in the world, and once she achieves that, she'll be able to enjoy life and move on.'

The message that Kirsty wanted the programme to convey to her son was more emotional: 'I would want to tell him that I love him very much, always have, that was never an issue at all. I didn't give him away because I didn't love him. I gave him away because I did love him. I suppose I did what I thought was right for him at the time, and I so hope that I was right.'

When children are adopted, they're effectively given a whole new identity. They don't just take on the surname of their new parents, but almost always are given a new first name too. As Kirsty knew, at the time information about the identity of the child's new family was strictly controlled and was impossible for a birth parent to obtain on their own. Following changes in the law some years ago, however, there was one way for the *Long Lost Family* team to help Kirsty. They worked very closely with a leading Adoption Support Agency, which was legally entitled to see confidential adoption records. Once they had discovered Kirsty's baby's new name, they could trace him. If successful, the professional intermediary working alongside the *Long Lost Family* team would contact him. They would need to obtain his permission before passing on his details to the team.

Kirsty's son was, amazingly, found to be living not too far from Kirsty. His name is James Sorrentino, and Nicky Campbell went to see him, to show him Kirsty's photograph and tell him a little bit about her. 'Not a day goes by when Kirsty doesn't think about James,' he said, 'but what about his perspective? I wonder if he's ever thought about his adoption at all, ever focused on it, ever seen a photograph of her? Does he want to meet his birth mother?'

James told Nicky that he was very surprised to hear from them, and to learn about Kirsty. He had known since he was seven that he was adopted, but he knew nothing of his birth mother at all. He said to Nicky, 'When I first received the letter, it came completely out of the blue. I was gobsmacked. It's incredible. It's the first time I ever knew what she was called, the first thing I think I ever really knew about her.'

James had never had a problem with being adopted. 'You forget about being adopted, and then all of a sudden you remember, and then you try not to think about it. I've had a great childhood. I love my mum and dad.' Because his sister was also adopted and didn't look like him, he never really felt that he was the 'odd one out'. When he saw how his friends had similar personalities to their parents', he would wonder where his roots were, where he came from. 'I don't have any grudges or anything like that. I hope she's not worried about that. I don't know if she'll be thinking, 'Is he going to hate me because I gave him up?' There's none of that.'

When he was younger, if people said to him, after hearing his name, 'You don't look very Italian,' he'd make an excuse, but as he grew older, he got to the point where he'd just say, 'That's because I'm adopted.' His attitude was that of someone comfortable in themselves. It wasn't a problem for him, so therefore it couldn't be a problem for anyone else.

Nicky offered to show him the photograph of Kirsty he'd brought with him. 'I'd love to see it. My heart's started thumping now. A big moment.' After a few moments, he smiled and said, 'It's so weird, looking at my mum . . . incredible.'

Nicky passed over the letter Kirsty had written to James.

Firstly, and most importantly, I hope this finds you happy and well . . . I've never stopped thinking about you and hoping you were happy. Over the past twenty-five years I've wondered how you were every birthday. I would love to meet you and see for myself the person you've grown into. Take care.

With fondest thoughts and wishes, Kirsty

James's reaction was immediate. 'That's a nice letter; I like that. It never occurred to me that she'd be thinking about me, especially on birthdays, wondering how I am. I just never thought about it. I definitely have to meet her now that I've read the letter and seen the picture. I can't let it lie now. I can't just stop at a picture — that doesn't answer any questions, does it?'

When James had first been approached by the professional intermediary working alongside the *Long Lost Family* team, the news had come as a real shock for him and he was taken aback. Although there was no doubt in his mind that he would reply to the letter, and that he wanted it to lead to a meeting with Kirsty, he was also concerned about the effect this would have on his family, and he thought long and hard about it before he even spoke to them. His adoptive parents supported his decision, and he now wanted to take this further. From his own experiences as a father, he was aware of how hard Kirsty must have found those early days.

It was then time for Davina to go and see Kirsty, to tell her James had been traced and that he wanted to meet her. Having Davina McCall in her house was exciting, but for Kirsty there was only one focus. 'I never had that star-struck business with her, because what we were doing was so much more important — for me, he's the star!' So the first thing Kirsty wanted to know after she was told they'd found James was 'Is he alright?' Davina reassured her, but Kirsty was so shocked — and so relieved — she had to ask again, as if she couldn't believe it. 'Is he?'

Kirsty was overwhelmed to see a photograph of James. It was obvious that she was so grateful to have this. She was so pleased to hear about him and see him, and couldn't quite believe that, after all the years during which she'd thought about him and felt pain over the decision she'd made to part with him, she was about to get a second chance.

The photograph James sent her made her laugh with delight. Since he was born, all she'd had were the two photographs of him as a baby, and no matter how hard she tried, she couldn't picture him grown up, so she was quite shocked to see what he looked like as an adult. 'Oh, wow! Oh, that's unbelievable. Oh, bless him, he's lovely, isn't he? He's got my eyes, hasn't he?' For a few moments she clasped the picture, drinking it in. 'I've wanted to see this picture for so long — twenty-five years. Oh, he's gorgeous, isn't he?'

To her surprise, Davina produced another photograph. This one showed James with his own son. At the sight of the two of them together, Kirsty clasped her hand to her mouth — she hadn't expected that at all. 'He's a daddy! Oh, wow! Oh, he's lovely.'

Davina had more for her — a letter James had written to her, to be passed on. Again, Kirsty was overwhelmed — so much news in such a short space of time after years of silence.

Hi Kirsty,

I hope you can read this, because my handwriting is terrible! I hope you are well.

My name is James. I live with my girlfriend and my little boy. We also have another baby on the way.

I have had a happy childhood and a good upbringing with very loving parents and an older sister. Being adopted has not caused me any problems, and I don't have any grudges. Since having my son, it made me realise it must have been so hard for you.

When I first received a letter saying that you wanted to find me I was very shocked and felt quite scared. I never thought I would ever meet you, but now the opportunity has arisen, I am curious to find out what you are like and to see if we have any similar traits of personality. I've never met someone that looks like me except for my son.

I don't know where the reunion will lead to or where I would like it to lead. We will just have to find out.

James

Kirsty found his letter 'really comforting. I've worried so much. Did I do the right thing? I was scared to death that he was unhappy and hated me for doing it in the first place.'

Davina asked Kirsty if she would like to take this a stage further and meet James. 'If it never went any further than this, I would be happy just to know. I'm really happy.' But . . . 'Oh, yes, I'd love to meet him. If I got the chance, it would be lovely.'

Kirsty was beaming with pleasure and delight. 'It's the best day. It's like all my birthdays and Christmases came at once. Lovely.'

Kirsty and James arranged to meet in a

park not far from the village where he'd lived with the foster family after he was born. Over the next few days, Kirsty read and re-read the letter he'd sent her, as well as carefully studying the pictures she'd been given. 'Looking at the photos they gave me kept me going until the day of the meeting.'

The reunion

It was the morning of her meeting with James, and Kirsty still couldn't stop pinching herself. 'It's hard to believe — a twenty-five-year dream coming true.' James too was excited: 'I'm definitely ready to meet her now. I don't have any worries anymore; I'm just excited to meet her, say hello, and find things out.' Nicky escorted him to the park and asked him what he wanted to say to Kirsty. 'I don't know. I don't know what to say or what to ask. I think Kirsty will know what to tell me about, what I'd want to know. There are a lot of questions I want answered — I'm really intrigued.'

When they arrived at the park, Davina said to Kirsty that it was weird to think James was already there, ready to greet her. Kirsty — who had for years hoped to see James in the street — agreed: 'It's very strange.'

Both of them were extremely nervous when

they finally saw each other. All the feelings brimming in Kirsty bubbled over, and she could barely push out the words, 'How lovely to see you.'

James too seemed taken aback by the intensity of the moment and replied, 'Hello. Nice to . . . er . . . nice to see you.' The two of them hugged each other.

This was the first time Kirsty had touched James. When he was a baby, she had resisted holding him, as she was worried she would never be able to let him go. 'It was amazing, actually holding him — something I'd been waiting for all that time.'

The first moments of the meeting were, for both of them, overwhelming. For Kirsty, her years of searching, leading to this moment, had left her almost exhausted by the emotion inside her. James, who wasn't used to seeing someone who looked like him, couldn't help but stare at her. They both acknowledged this was a 'crazy' situation, and started to slowly relax.

'I am so glad that you didn't say no to this meeting,' Kirsty said. James reassured her that he couldn't have done so, but Kirsty — still unable to believe that her son was sitting in front of her — said she'd thought he might. James was adamant, and said, 'No, I couldn't. You can't have this letter saying your birth mum wants to meet you and then turn your back on it because you'd just be thinking about it all the time.'

'Thank you for that,' Kirsty said, 'because it has made such a massive difference, it really has. God — I can't believe you're sitting there. Wow. Shall we go for a walk?'

The two of them walked away from the bench where they'd been sitting, and headed down towards the café by the car park at the edge of the park. Both Andy and James's partner Clare were there, waiting to meet them. On the way, Kirsty said, 'This day has totally changed my life, completely. I've got hope now that I never believed that I would have. Hopefully it's just the beginning.'

For James, 'That section of my life just seemed a mystery, something not known, just a blank spot in my past. That's now kind of been filled.'

They carried on heading down towards the café. Kirsty asked, 'So what are you thinking now? Are you hungry?' Later she would find out that James is always hungry!

After the programme

In the café, once filming was over and James had had something to eat, the two of them sat with Andy and Clare and talked. They discovered then how close to an accidental meeting they'd come. Andy flies microlight aircraft, and just the previous weekend he'd met someone at the club who he'd introduced Kirsty to. Andy mentioned his passion, and James said, 'Oh, there's a guy who lives next door to us who flies microlights. He's a friend of mine — we go to the pub together.' It was, of course, the same person. This naturally sparked a conversation about other times when Kirsty and James's paths could have crossed — they both went to Milton Keynes regularly, for example.

Clare warned Kirsty during their chat that James was notoriously bad at replying to messages. Despite her advice, Kirsty initially found this very hard to deal with; after years of searching for her son, to have finally found him and then not to hear back from him when she called or texted was difficult for her. At first she'd imagine all sorts of things, inventing all sorts of reasons why she didn't get a message back, because she was so used to disappointment that this seemed to be part of her way of thinking.

One enormous change for her happened almost overnight. The nervousness she felt when she went away from her home — the panic attacks that had curtailed some of her social life — vanished. Quite why this was the case, Kirsty wasn't sure. She thought that it was probably because she was no longer hoping to catch sight of her son when she was walking about in a crowd, that the impulse to look into the faces of all the young men passing by on the street had gone. Within that overpowering feeling had been a fear — a fear that he might pass her by unnoticed. Once that fear was removed, and the impulse gone, Kirsty felt the anxiety drop off her shoulders like a coat being removed. 'I didn't realise that was what was causing it till it went away. I can go out and do things again, and socialise without panicking. I've been able to do lots of things since then that I'd never have dreamed of some months ago. That was something nice to nip in the bud.'

However, it has left her feeling vulnerable in other ways: 'I'm more emotional than I was. I get more emotional about things.' So when she doesn't see James for a while, her anxiety rises up again. She has realised this and has started to deal with it, so that she can manage better when she hasn't seen him. 'It's started not to feel like such a long time now. A week used to feel like absolutely ages — it was agony — but then I managed nine weeks. I'm getting better in that respect. I don't need to see him quite so much.'

On one of the occasions they met up, they went for a walk, taking Kirsty's dog with them. Kirsty told him that she used to look into the faces of young men passing by, and how she thought she must have spooked them a bit. James laughed and said that they probably went home feeling rather excited that they'd been 'checked out' by this woman in town. He himself had done that a little bit, he said. They wondered whether they would have recognised each other; Kirsty was in no doubt that she would have.

Later during their walk, she could sense James studying her as she walked beside him. 'He was laughing. I asked him why, and he said, 'We've got the same profile.' That was fascinating for him.'

That James never looked like anybody till his son was born, and then to be standing in front of an adult who looked so much like him 'was quite something for him, I think,' said Kirsty. 'Even if he did keep laughing at first. We look alike. That was weird for a bit, looking at somebody when it was almost like looking in a mirror. Of course, I love that.' Kirsty's also picked up on one or two other physical traits that they share, their body language being one example. 'When we sit talking, we both fidget in the same way.' But they are like chalk and cheese in other ways.

They compared notes on how the process of making the programme had been for them. Kirsty had taken advice from the *Long Lost Family* team, the adoption experts and the professional intermediaries involved when she wrote her initial letter to James, ensuring that what he finally read had been trimmed down to include only the sort of information that he would need in a first letter. James, on the other hand, wrote his letter without any guidance.

Kirsty told James all the things she had done in trying to find him herself. James said he had wondered about a few questions that no one else could answer for him, such as inherited health conditions. She asked him if he would have replied to the advert she'd placed on the message board forum if he'd seen it, and he assured her he would have done. Of course he hadn't seen it because he'd been looking under his adopted name, which Kirsty had never known, and he hadn't put his date of birth in, which would have been automatically linked to the date she put in her advert. Despite all the effort they had both made to find each other, Kirsty thinks that, for James, the urgency that she felt wasn't there — 'It wasn't like it was for me, that's for sure.'

Kirsty had read as much as she could

about how to deal with reunions, and she had spoken to professionals as well. The *Long Lost Family* team had ensured that throughout this process she was supported and advised by adoption and reunion experts, as well as the professional intermediaries they had both worked with. Between them, the professionals had many years of experience in helping to arrange and manage reunions between birth mothers and their adopted children. However, every situation is different and when Kirsty met James, what she thought she knew was forgotten. 'I managed to hold myself together for the first couple of meetings. There was quite a lot of deep conversation in the beginning. I told him how it all happened — he wanted to know everything.' This seemed very positive to her, as the professionals she had spoken to told her this was quite unusual, that to get to this stage usually took many months of meetings between the people involved.

The speed at which things moved brought with it different expectations for them both. The process of getting to know each other happened so quickly — 'It was a bit of a whirlwind, I suppose,' said Kirsty. 'That initial euphoria sweeps you off your feet.'

Kirsty has always been open about her feelings, and remains so. Since she was reunited with James, she has found that the traumatic days of his birth and the weeks that followed are no longer a subject her family don't discuss. 'We talk more than ever, and have covered a lot of things. Things have come out. I found out a lot of things I didn't know about how other people feel. It's been good for us to be able to talk about it.' She has also found it helpful to talk to people who have been in a similar situation to her own, including some of the other participants on the *Long Lost Family* programmes. While their stories are different, they have a perspective that helps Kirsty to understand her own situation. Speaking to someone who has a relationship with an adoptive parent that they don't wish to change has helped her enormously.

James made one request of Kirsty at that meeting: 'I said to him, 'Is there anything you want to ask me?' and the first thing was 'Who was my dad?' It was obviously quite important to him to know.' Kirsty hadn't spoken to him since she was fifteen, and she wasn't even sure she knew how to get hold of him, but she thought it was possible that he would watch the programme and recognise her, so she had planned to contact him before the programme was screened, even before James asked her for more information about him. 'It was only fair to let him know, in case he put two and two together when he saw it on the TV. That would have been really quite cruel. I didn't want that to happen.' She knew that she would have to track him down and break the momentous news to him — that all those years ago, after the two of them had split up, she'd given birth to a son who'd been adopted.

Kirsty was able to find him after a few days' searching. He hadn't left the area he'd lived in back then, and when she found a man there with the right name and the right birth date, she was sure she'd found him. She was advised not to approach him herself, however, but to go through an intermediary. The intermediary wrote to him, asking if he remembered Kirsty, and said that she was seeking contact with people in her past. If he was the person she remembered, perhaps he would ring this number? He rang the intermediary, who explained why Kirsty wanted to contact him — which obviously came as a huge surprise and shock to him.

When he subsequently spoke to Kirsty, the following day, after he'd told his wife the news, he said that when he'd opened the letter he'd remembered her right away, and assumed that she was getting in touch because she had a terminal illness. 'It was a huge relief to me to talk to him. I could explain exactly what had happened, because he didn't know any of it, of course. That was a weight off my shoulders. In the end, he was quite excited about it, so it went quite well.' She was initially taken aback when she first spoke to him, as he sounded just like James — she had forgotten that before she heard his voice. Subsequently he and his family met James.

Meanwhile Kirsty found herself struggling with each development. Everything had happened so fast and the realisation of her goal — finding James — left her without a defined aim, as she hadn't envisaged what would happen after their first meeting. The idea of finding him had been such an all-consuming one for her that she hadn't had time to think about what it would mean for her — or for him — and now that came to the front of her mind. She remained excited at finding her son, but it was a lot for James to absorb at a very busy time in his life — not only was he meeting his birth mother and, a little later on, his father, but at the same time he and Clare were anticipating the birth of their second child.

Despite the fact that she'd done a lot of reading in preparation, and that she'd had sessions with the *Long Lost Family* psychologist, as well as support from the adoption and reunion experts and other experienced professional intermediaries who worked with the *Long Lost Family* team, after a while Kirsty realised that what she'd read no longer applied to her situation. 'You're all level-headed and you think you've got it all sorted out, and you accept they've got this other family — but in reality, when you meet that person and the emotions take over, everything, all rational thinking, goes out of the window. I've carried on being open about my feelings, whereas things have calmed down for him. The excitement is not the same for him, but for me, it still is.'

During the early days of filming, word had got back to Kirsty's parents of what she was doing, and they decided not to watch the programme till they had themselves met James. They met in a pub for lunch. 'It was all light-hearted, and nothing heavy was talked about.' Another barrier had been broken, but that didn't mean that things would run smoothly as a result.

Kirsty's sister, meanwhile, watched the programme and was very moved by it. Kirsty and Andy had, along with James and Clare, watched a screening of the programme before it was aired. 'It was weird. I was more shocked at looking at myself on screen than anything else. It wasn't till I watched it at home that I properly took it all in. It makes me smile. It's nice to see James sitting there chatting.'

Other people's reactions to the programme were varied. There were some who felt Kirsty talked about her feelings more than James's, or anyone else's, but she pointed out to them that the programme followed her story, so naturally it was her feelings that were most talked about. She has noticed that when she and James are out and about, it is James who is recognised more often. Kirsty would very much like to be able to use her experiences to help others in a similar situation — perhaps that opportunity will come once things, for her, have settled down a bit.

On her birthday, she and James went out for lunch together. Later on in the year they celebrated around the time of his birthday — she'd marked the occasion privately every year since he was born, so it was great for her to be able to see him close to that day. She wanted to give him a present of a driving experience at Silverstone, and James said he'd like it if she came too — so the pair of them went along for the day and had a fabulous time out on the track.

Once the programme was aired, Kirsty

found it easier to talk to people about the issues that had troubled her for so long in her life and that until then she'd kept private. She'd never had any difficulty discussing things with Andy, but for people who didn't know her background, the TV programme came as a surprise. When she went back to work, people who in the past had explained at length how agonising childbirth was for them, rushed up to her and said, 'I can't believe I told you this and you didn't say anything. I went on and on and you already knew!'

Most complex, inevitably, has been the situation with James's adoptive family. Kirsty has nothing but gratitude toward them and would love the opportunity to meet them, to tell them how glad she is that James is their son, but perhaps understandably this hasn't happened, at least not yet. 'I wrote to them, shortly after we first met, to put their minds at ease, to reassure them that I wasn't trying to take him away, to thank them — I did that off my own bat. James told me they appreciated it.' It's easy for Kirsty to see why they might be reluctant to meet her, and she fully appreciates that the thought of someone coming into her family, turning up uninvited, is not something she'd want either. 'I felt guilty about that, wondered if I'd caused them any pain. I felt bad that I might be causing turmoil in their house. That's an awful thought — I didn't want to cause anyone any pain. That reluctance was there even when I was searching for him. It was something I always worried about, and then when our meeting actually happened, and I realised it was difficult for his parents, I felt terrible, really bad. What they maybe don't realise is that I am not a threat to them — she is his mum and he is his dad, and they always will be.'

There are guidelines that have been written to try to make sense of the relationship between a birth mother and her adopted son. Kirsty has read them all, even though she quickly realised they weren't all going to apply to her — but there don't seem to be any at all that help in dealing with the relationship with the adoptive parents. For Kirsty and James, this is something that has to be worked out by themselves, and Kirsty would like to do more to help, but knows that she cannot — that she has to stand back and let it sort itself out. All sorts of thoughts have come to her, such as her age counting against her, as she is closer in age to James than his parents, but as Kirsty says, 'I make a lot of assumptions, and they're probably wrong, which is why it would be nice to meet them and get that out of the way, to know what everybody is thinking. They're probably like me, imagining things that aren't happening. But I've got to let him deal with that.'

They both have so much to deal with. When they first met, they were offered support but, as Kirsty says, 'You're so carried away with the excitement — and he was excited as well — I felt there wasn't anything I needed to talk about. As time's gone on and things have started to settle, reality's kicking in.' Such an upheaval in anyone's life needs careful handling, and Kirsty is finding avenues of her own in order to explore her feelings since the reunion took place. Both were offered professional psychological support by the *Long Lost Family* team, the adoption and reunion experts and the professional intermediaries who worked closely with them. Kirsty continues to receive support from them.

'A lot of people don't understand how complex the whole thing is. We're lucky in that we are living fairly close together, but in some ways, people in our situation who live further away from each other have more quality time together, whereas James and I can get together and we'll just have a couple of hours in the pub.'

Kirsty's aware that she sometimes overthinks situations, and that maybe things aren't always as she imagines them to be, and she is ready to admit to being 'an emotional bag', carrying around long-suppressed feelings of guilt, among others. 'I do tend to over-analyse things, worry about things that aren't happening. I'd buried a lot of feelings, and got used to not showing them — and I'd always been quite private, on this subject anyway. All through the filming I didn't cry or anything — even when I met him, I didn't cry. Then all the emotions started to come out, stuff that I'd almost forgotten and hadn't dealt with them back then, and I had to cope with everything in one go. I've dealt with them since, which has been quite difficult at times.

'I'm more emotional; I get more upset now. I'm quite controlled normally, so it's more to do with James than anything else. I can't control my emotions around him — I feel out of control, and one word from him can make or break my day. He's got that power over me, emotionally, without wanting it. He tells me it's better for me to get my feelings off my chest than to stew about them. Then I shrug and smile at him and say, 'Oh, you know what I'm like.' He makes me feel less emotionally secure.'

In some ways, of course, this is no different from the experiences of a parent of a new-born baby who realises that they are now linked to someone else's life forever. For Kirsty, this has come about late in life, so of course the experience for her is different. 'Not having that history makes it harder. But I don't regret it. I don't want to go back to how it was before I met him. I was lucky in that my son had no issues with me, but in some ways the fact that he's sorted is harder. Of course he's had a huge amount to deal with in the past year, what with the new baby and everything; there's been a huge amount for him to absorb.'

The only advice she feels she can offer anyone else in her situation is to be patient. 'Such a big word; I've used it so many times. Unless you're very lucky, it's not going to be how you imagine. You can have all these fantasies, but you've got to come back to reality eventually. Meeting the person you've been searching for doesn't solve your problems at all. It answers a few questions, but then it opens the floodgates, and you end up with all this emotion. I found myself grieving for all that I'd missed over the years. I've seen a few photos of him as he was growing up and, lovely as they are, they broke my heart. I missed all of that. That brought home to me how big the whole thing was; it was one of the first hurdles I had to get over, and I know that there will be another one, and then another. Just when you think you're getting there, something else rocks your boat. I read before I met James that the reunion isn't about that one day; it can take years. I didn't understand that at the time, but I certainly do now. It isn't something that starts and stops on that first day. You've got so much to get through. Nothing can prepare you for it actually happening. Nothing anyone can say will prepare you. Every situation is different.'

All Kirsty wants is one very simple thing: to love her son. That's it. Why that should be so difficult, so fraught with problems, is the question she wrestles with. 'I was foolish to think that finding him would be the end of all my problems. The only time I feel a bit better is when we're together, because then I can see the way he looks at me, the way he is with me. I quickly forget that when we're apart.

'I have a list of issues as long as my arm that I've had to get my head around and learn to live with. I think it's going to go alright, but I don't think it's going to go the way that perhaps I'd wanted it to before I met him. I know he's there, which is the good thing. At the beginning, I went into it just wanting to know he was alright and happy, and I was really happy to find out that he was. But then

I met him and his family and started forming a relationship, and I totally fell in love with him, as a mother, and I can't turn it off.

'It's definitely going to be a long road, and whether I will ever feel totally satisfied, I don't know. I go through little stages; I feel better, then something happens and — BANG! — I go back a few steps again. I'm hanging on, with everything I've got. I've just got to try to learn patience — it's not easy.'

7

Laura, Hunting for Her Birth Mother

'When you're fifteen, you don't think your parents have feelings. At the end of the day, where would I be without them?'

Laura McCarthy grew up knowing she had been adopted. She lived in a small village with her parents and her adopted brother. Laura was always restless, and found the area she lived in confining; life in the village seemed too slow, and even the world beyond it didn't appear to be exciting enough. To feel restricted in this way was something Laura's parents didn't seem, to her, to understand, and there was a lot of friction in the house when she was a teenager.

Eventually, when she was sixteen and a half, she left home. Initially she moved to the nearby city of Oxford, but that didn't offer her enough, and soon she had moved to London. From there, she started travelling, working in France and Greece, before heading to the other side of the world and, at the age of twenty-three, settling in Australia.

Despite knowing she'd miss her family, she was happy to make a home over there. 'I felt oppressed living in the UK; I didn't fit in. I never thought I was different, just that everyone else was boring.'

Laura always wanted to know about the circumstances of her birth, about why she was adopted, and — most of all — about her birth mother. She learned not to ask questions about this at home, which only added to her frustration. Laura wanted to talk about things, but it seemed nobody else did. It would be many years before she found out why.

Even at a very young age, Laura had decided she would look for her birth mother. As soon as she reached eighteen, she asked to see her adoption file. 'There was a process to follow. I had to see a councillor before I was given The File. It was ceremoniously opened — and it had nothing in it.'

This was a devastating moment for her. 'I do remember them saying that if my biological mother had wanted to be found at a later date then she had the opportunity to put something in that file, to be read when I was eighteen.' To discover it was empty meant that Laura's birth mother probably didn't want or expect to be found, and therefore didn't want or expect contact with her biological daughter.

The only information Laura was able to glean from the file was her birth mother's name — Linda Williamson — and her date of birth. From this, she learned that Linda had been fifteen when she had conceived Laura.

With so few facts to go on, Laura's imagination took over. She imagined an innocent young girl, running barefoot through the meadows, perhaps an unwilling victim of circumstance. In her mind, Laura began to develop a fairytale, that one day she would meet this unhappy woman, and 'put my arms round her, assuming that she'd felt guilty all these years'. Laura wanted to thank Linda for going through all that struggle and pain, and to tell her that something good had come from it all. She was full of sympathy for someone whom she thought most likely had been wronged. 'I can't imagine how difficult it must have been in 1966 for a fifteen- or sixteen-year-old to have gone through what she had to go through, and I wanted to meet my biological mother to tell her that. That in no way should she feel any blame or any guilt or anything negative about what she had to do.'

In the meantime, with nothing else to go on, Laura had to respect her birth mother's apparent wishes to be left alone, and to be content with her fairytale. Perhaps, she reasoned, her birth mother had reasons not to want to be found, and thoughts like this added to the picture of an unhappy innocent in Laura's mind. Things changed for her when she gave birth to her son Max. 'I gave birth and the next day I thought, 'As soon as I get out of here, I have to do something about the search.' I just realised how important that blood link is — Max is the only person on the planet who looks like me, who's like me, and it really brought home to me how much I wanted to find my other family.'

It wasn't just about wanting to meet someone she was related to by blood; it wasn't just about hoping to find someone whom she might resemble — it was also about her genetic inheritance. To an adopted child, the need to understand which aspects of their character come from their adoptive parents, and which come from their birth parents can be acute. Most families are prone to remarks like, 'Oh, you're just like your uncle Jimmy,' or, 'You take after your father in that respect.' But to an adopted child, knowing which character traits are inherited and which are nurtured can be vitally important. It's not just because an adopted child wants to know there's a connection going back into their past — they also want to understand themselves, and to know who they are. For Laura, this impulse grew stronger as she tried to track down Linda Williamson.

To aid her in her search, Laura employed an international search agency, as well as contacting Social Services. They were able to unearth more details for Laura, including Linda's birth certificate and a more complete record of Laura's own birth details: Laura had been born in a Mother and Baby Home in Northampton called St Saviours. They also learned that after giving Laura up for adoption, Linda had married a few years later.

To Laura's frustration and despair, however, the trail went cold at that point. The only people it led to didn't seem related to Linda in any way. Laura was unable to find out any more details, and the agencies she approached were unable to tell her any more. Every route she tried ended in failure. Once more, she had to bury her need to search for her birth mother for the moment.

Meanwhile, she would read every article about adoption she came across and would watch avidly any programme on TV. After a long time, one such programme sparked her interest in the search all over again. Even though Laura felt fed up, after hunting for so long, she felt this was one opportunity she couldn't ignore. 'I knew my mum, if she was still with us, would be in her sixties now. This was my last chance.' Her application led her to the researchers of *Long Lost Family*.

Before she went ahead with the programme, Laura felt she needed to tell her family back at home in the UK. Her adoptive father was supportive of her decision to look for her birth parent, but urged Laura to be aware of how the news would affect her mother. Both her adoptive mother and her brother were less keen that she go ahead, but Laura felt she had no choice anymore — it was a journey she needed to complete. She wasn't happy that they felt this way, but, 'At the end of the day, it's my birth story, and it is what it is.' Even though Linda had given her up for adoption, even though she'd placed nothing in the file for Laura to find, the urge for Laura to know something of her birth mother was too strong. 'Not knowing is the hardest thing to live with. Not knowing if she's ever thought about me, not knowing if she has blocked me out of her mind, not knowing what happened to her afterwards . . . '

The *Long Lost Family* research team was able to establish the reasons why Laura had not managed to locate Linda. There were errors in the transcription of her birth certificate, which stemmed from the hand-writing on it. The curls on one numeral had been misread, turning a seven into a nine, and so both Linda and Laura's birthdays had been incorrectly passed on. This was one reason why Laura had never managed to get very far in tracing her birth mother.

There was another reason, and it wasn't one that Laura wanted to hear. Linda was traced to the United States, but she had died there many years before. She had become very ill with lung cancer, and although she'd made a recovery, she'd returned to hospital following a stroke. She decided that she no longer wished to carry on receiving treatment and, as she had become strongly religious in her last few years, felt she wanted to die, as she believed she would meet God. The machines sustaining her life were turned off at her request, and Linda had died at almost exactly the same time all those years ago that Laura had stopped her search. The professional intermediary who worked closely alongside the *Long Lost Family* team had to tell Laura the sad news.

The phone call devastated Laura, and she sobbed and sobbed. 'I felt so let down — all those years I'd been looking, and I'd stopped searching just about the time she'd died.'

They had more to tell Laura — a little bit about Linda's life and some good news about other family members — but that day wasn't the right time to talk to her about it.

Once Laura had got over the shock, she was able to take in a bit more about her birth mother's life. Nicky Campbell made the trip to see her, taking with him some things that would come as a surprise to her. Laura told him that she'd found the whole experience hard, and that she wished she'd got this far earlier, so that she could have made contact with Linda herself. She still held her belief that Linda had been an innocent soul, and this made her sadder still: 'I've been thinking about how she had such a short life.'

Nicky was able to produce a photograph of Linda, the first glimpse Laura had ever had of her birth mother. The photograph stunned her: 'She is beautiful. I think I've got her eyes.' To see someone who looked so like her was astonishing to Laura, who felt she had spent her whole life waiting to see someone who did. The whole experience was something she found very difficult to cope with, because she felt as if she were standing outside herself, watching the whole thing happen to her. Perhaps this was because she'd been waiting for this moment for so long, and had never thought it would happen, and the intensity of the feeling was something she could only cope with by distancing herself from it. At the same time, she was acutely conscious of the conflicting sensations it was creating in her, and she didn't know whether to laugh or cry. 'I was a mess,' she said later, 'and I felt every emotion possible running through me.'

And Nicky had more news for Laura. The picture had come from Alison, Linda's other daughter. Nicky had a photograph of her, and told Laura that Alison had expressed a wish that Laura had always been happy. At the sight of her picture, Laura's tears flowed even more freely. 'My baby sister. Gorgeous.' Alison's own reaction to the photograph of Laura that she'd seen had been similar — 'She's gorgeous. I can see Linda in her as well.'

Alison had been able to give the *Long Lost Family* team some details about Linda, which Nicky could pass on to Laura. Alison, born two years after Laura, had always known she had a half-sister, as her mother had never hidden anything about Laura from her. Alison had always wanted a big sister, and on special days — in particular on her wedding day and when her own children were born — had wished that her big sister could be there with her. 'When I was little I used to wish she was here so I could play with her, tell her secrets. She's always been a part of my life, always.' The news that Laura had been fruitlessly searching for them for so long was sad for Alison, as she herself had been prevented from looking for her half-sister for many years by the laws governing adoption, but she was so excited that the big sister she'd always dreamed about was now fully in her life.

Linda's story was more complex than Laura had first understood, and that meant that Alison was able to understand Laura's situation more than Laura knew. When Alison was four years old, Linda left her and her father. Alison's father was married again, to one of Linda's sisters, and they brought Alison up together. Linda visited, but only infrequently. Alison grew up knowing that Linda was her mother, but said that 'It wasn't a typical mother-daughter relationship; we were apart for such a long time.' She came to feel that Linda was more of an aunt to her. When Alison explained this, she said, 'I feel like Laura and I have got a bond, because Linda left me as well. I feel we've got that in common, as well as being sisters.'

By the time Alison was a teenager, Linda had moved to America, and so contact between the two of them lessened, but when

Linda was gravely ill Alison spent quite a lot of time with her before she died. As a child, Alison did resent her mother's absences, but once she had a family of her own she found it easier to forgive Linda. She was aware that Linda was gregarious and outgoing, but also strong-minded and independent.

Alison had written Laura a letter, which Nicky passed over.

Dear Laura,

After so many imagined conversations with you in my head, to know you are actually going to read these words fills me with joy!

Ever since I was a little girl I have known I had a big sister and I used to wish you were there to play dolls with and tell secrets to.

Laura, I know you must have been incredibly sad to know that Linda is no longer with us. I know that she would have been so pleased that you'd found your family, and through us you will learn about the person she was. I remember she once told me that if you ever came to find her, she would be so happy to see you, and eager to learn about the life you'd had. Most of all, she'd have wanted to know that you had been happy and loved.

I'm sure, like me, you are full of so many emotions. I'm excited, nervous, but most of all so happy that finally we are going to meet! My husband and children and all your aunts, uncles and cousins are also extremely excited and can't wait to welcome you into the family. We have so much time to make up for, so as I come to the end of this letter, I'm excited that this is just the beginning.

See you soon!

Love, Alison

The letter prompted more tears from Laura, who was thrilled by Alison's words. 'I would so love to meet her. I'm so happy.'

It was suggested to Laura that she write back to Alison, something she found a struggle. Not because she didn't want to, and not because she couldn't think of something to say. It was the opposite problem for her — 'How do you put forty-five years of life on to one sheet of A4?'

She drafted her letter, but was unsure if it said all the right things. So she asked her son to read it, to make sure she'd said what she needed to say, and in the best possible way. To help him, she gave him Alison's letter as well, so that he could compare what each had said.

Max looked at both sheets for a while, then turned to look up at Laura, puzzled. 'Which one's which, Mum?' he asked. It wasn't just the handwriting that confused him. The words Laura had chosen, the phrases she'd used, were identical to the ones Alison had put in her letter. Laura studied the two letters herself, and realised that Max was right. Almost immediately, she felt this was a pretty good thing — that there was a connection already forming between her sister and herself that she hadn't even noticed. It took someone else to see it. 'That meant a lot to me,' said Laura.

The reunion

The next stage for Laura was to fly over to the UK to meet Alison for the first time. The two of them met in the place in Northampton where Linda had given birth to Laura; it was no longer a Mother and Baby Home — it was now a convent — but they were happy to welcome the two women in for their first meeting.

Understandably, Laura grew more nervous as the time approached. 'It's so weird,' she told Nicky Campbell. 'This person is a blood relation of mine, and until today the only blood relative I had was my own child. It's really strange; it's just the hugest thing that's ever happened to me.' Mingled with her excitement was anxiety. 'Am I going to be everything she's hoped and dreamed about? She's been thinking about me for forty years — maybe I'm not going to match up. I'm scared she'll be disappointed.' If she had only known what was going through Alison's mind, she'd have been greatly reassured. Alison was also edgy, because all her life she had dreamt of having an older sister — and now she was about to meet her. 'I hope we're going to be friends as well as sisters,' she said.

With snow on the ground, it was a far cry from Laura's home in Sydney, where it was summertime. Walking through the front door of the convent was a poignant moment for Laura because, as Nicky Campbell pointed out, it was the first time she had ever been somewhere where she knew her birth mother had been too. When Laura was born, she and Linda had been together in the home for four weeks before she was taken away to be adopted. 'I just hope she was happy,' Laura replied. 'I hope she was okay. It feels like a happy house to me. I feel she's here, you know — and I don't believe in all that stuff, but I feel she's here.' Shortly after, Nicky left her alone to meet Alison. Laura could barely contain herself as she waited. When she caught sight of Alison approaching the front door of the convent, she jumped up to meet her, and the two threw their arms around each other, laughing with delight and surprise before their tears took over. 'I can't believe it,' they both managed to stutter out.

Alison straight away told Laura that she looked like Linda and had the same facial expressions, and that Laura would be able to see this family resemblance for herself when she met their auntie Carol.

The concerns Laura had always had when she was growing up, about her birth mother and what she was thinking and going through, were quickly laid to rest by Alison. She confirmed everything she'd said to Laura in her letter: 'I've always known about you, and I've always known you were going to come and find us. Always.' The words brought more tears from both of them.

'The most wonderful thing for me,' Laura told her, 'was to hear you've always known about me, and always wanted to meet me, because I never thought it would be like this. I always assumed I was this little thing no one wanted to talk about . . . ' In the past, Laura explained, she had never felt able to talk about her adoption with her family in the UK, and because it wasn't something she was able to discuss with them, she felt it was some sort of dirty secret.

Alison was clear in her reply. 'You were

never a dirty little secret. We always knew about you, we just hoped one day you'd come and find us. Auntie Carol said Linda was always wondering what you were up to, and how you were getting on. I feel a bond with you already because she wasn't really there much for me either.'

Laura added, 'You grew up without her too,' to which Alison replied, 'I think she made mistakes when she was younger. Had you turned up when she was alive, she'd have welcomed you with open arms.'

There was one other thing Laura wanted to say right away. Something in the letter Alison had written had struck a real chord with her, and she wanted Alison to know how much it had meant to her. 'In your letter you wrote that you couldn't wait to welcome me into the family. I really hung on to that word: 'the' family, not 'our' family. It wasn't like you were saying it was your family; you just said it like I was already in the family.'

Alison — who had known that Laura would pick up on this word in that way, and had included it especially — rushed to reassure her: 'You are, its just you haven't met all of us yet.'

Laura struggled on through her tears to say what she really wanted to: 'I'm really sorry Linda has passed away, but you have changed my life by saying that. That's more than I could possibly have hoped for.'

After the programme

Alison introduced Laura to her family, and in particular her father, who had of course married Linda, and was able to tell Laura an awful lot about her. 'He was lovely to me. He was very nice and very open.' It was thanks to him, and to conversations with other family members, that Laura was able to piece together more of Linda's story. She learned that Linda had had two sisters, that all three of them had had difficult childhoods — it sounded as if their home life had been very disruptive. At some stage, Linda had been taken into foster care. As the three sisters grew up, they had all become difficult to control.

Some parts of Linda's life chimed very much with Laura's own experiences. Laura had left home for work and to travel, and she discovered that when Linda had left, she too had travelled in a similar way, before settling in America. Laura began to form a picture of Linda as a strong-minded and independent woman, which was at odds with the vision she'd held for so long.

So one thing that changed as Laura found out more about her birth mother was her romantic view of her. She said, 'I don't know if I would have got on with Linda.' What she uncovered suggested a streak of selfishness in Linda, and Laura learned that Linda managed to hurt a few people. Even thirty years later, those wounds hadn't healed. It was clear that Linda had found it easy to manipulate people when she was younger, men in particular. Once she moved to America, and especially in her last years, it was clear that she had changed, and it's possible that she regretted her earlier behaviour — but Laura will never know that for certain.

'All my life I'd had it in my head that she'd been an innocent young girl, taken advantage of. The reality was just about the opposite.' This disappointed Laura because she had hoped to learn positive things about Linda, so that her own sense of self would be buoyed up as a result. 'When you're adopted, you want to find out where your character traits come from. When the fairytale was dashed, it seemed to me to mean that all the darker sides of my character were from Linda. That's been hard to adjust to, but a relief as well. I've had issues in my life, and I could never work out what was wrong, and it turns out that Linda had issues too, and never seemed to be totally happy. Maybe that's why I'm like that then. It really hadn't occurred to me that I might inherit dark stuff rather than good stuff from her, but it's been good to have this genetic disposition sorted out in my mind.'

It turned out that the situation was more problematic than that. Laura's parents, when they'd adopted her, had been warned about Linda's background — although they weren't given any specific details — and they had been advised not to discuss this with Laura under any circumstances when she was growing up. Laura feels that she now understands something about her adoptive mother and father: 'What can you do when you're handed this young child, barely six weeks old, and told to do this? I did the same when I had my son — I did as I was told to do.'

As a young girl, Laura had felt many times that she wasn't given the chance to discuss her adoption, and she finally knows why. All the experience she herself now had as a parent brought her to the realisation of just how hard it must have been for her mum and dad when Laura was demanding information about Linda: 'You don't think of it when you're fifteen — you don't think your parents have feelings. I was a horrible teenager, and

I'd say things just to push their buttons, to cut them to the quick.'

Looking for her birth mother has brought Laura the extraordinary comfort of a sister to whom she's already really close, but she is more conscious than ever of what her adoptive mother and father did for her, and how hard it must have been for them at times. 'At the end of the day, where would I be without them?'

Today, her relationship with Alison is an amazing one. The two of them are very close and in autumn 2011 travelled together to the United States not only to visit Linda's grave and her sister there, but also to have a holiday together. Laura readily admits that she's not easy on holidays. She doesn't want to lounge about by the pool reading, but wants to be busy. When planning the trip, she worried about whether she and Alison would be compatible. Would she make arrangements that would suit her, but not her sister?

In the end, it couldn't have been easier, because everything Laura planned turned out to be exactly what Alison liked.

'The way I feel now is that Alison and I are so close, though we hardly know each other. I've never had that feeling before. I grew up with my brother, we were good mates, but the way I feel about Alison is more like the way I love my son. It's hard to describe. There is something about blood that makes it feel different. It's like a secret code that only you two can understand. The way you talk, do things — the other person just gets it. They understand it. I feel that with her, and the only other person I feel that with is my son.'

8

Sarah, Searching for Her Birth Mother

'How could I be that lucky? I couldn't believe it. I just felt extraordinarily lucky, thrilled, and so happy. So happy.'

Sarah's dad was an estate agent and her mum, a part-time hairdresser, stayed at home. Her childhood was fantastic — Sarah remembers it as idyllic — with holidays and horse-riding featuring high in her memory. She had two brothers, the eldest, like her, was adopted, but then her mother had a baby, even though she and Sarah's father had been told they'd never have children. Sarah was only five but, to her, there wasn't 'a massive change' in family life — just pleasure in having a younger child in the home.

Sarah had always known she was adopted. Her parents had made no secret of it. She had come to them 'with lots of nice clothes with me.' (Lots of mothers placed parcels of clothes with their child before they were given up for adoption; one worker in a home recalled this practice as 'the last thing they could do for their babies'.) The story her parents told Sarah made her adoption seem as if it was something special, 'as if they'd chosen me. I had this fairytale image in my head, and while now I realise they didn't go into a ward full of babies and say, 'We'll have that one,' as a child I thought that's what had happened. I believed I had been picked out.' Being adopted wasn't something that really troubled Sarah when she was growing up; it was just a fact.

Sarah did feel a little bit different from the rest of her family. 'I don't look like my mum and dad, and I'm not like them.' It wasn't just a physical thing, although Sarah is shorter than the rest of her family; it was also her personality — she always felt she was louder than them. However, it didn't concern her too much — 'Not everyone looks like their mum and dad anyway, do they?'

Sarah's upbringing was so happy that she has brought her own children up exactly as she and her brothers were. 'I've copied my mother exactly: firm but fair, loving but not a pushover. She did a good job, and I've tried to do the same. I've had her on a pedestal all of my life, and refer to her better judgement on everything. She's the only person I trust more than I trust myself.'

The issue of Sarah's adoption rarely arose.

When Sarah asked, the only information she got was that her birth mother had been a single woman, and that giving Sarah up for adoption 'was what you did' in those circumstances. At the time, Sarah didn't feel that she needed to know any more. She had only a hazy idea of the woman who'd given her up; she didn't spend time imagining what she was like or anything. If she did think about what she might be like, 'I put my own face to her, an older version of me.' Sarah's happy family life carried on, even through her tempestuous teenage years. 'Obviously everyone has a tricky time when they are a teenager, and Mum said I was a nightmare. I just really wanted to do what I wanted to do.'

While for some the desire to find their birth relative is a constant ache, for Sarah it was different. 'I had this huge curiosity that I couldn't get rid of, about the person I was related to,' but it wasn't something that she thought about every day. Sarah didn't like telling anyone she was adopted, not because she was ashamed of it, but because it didn't seem to her to have the importance other people gave to it — and she didn't feel it should define her. So it wasn't until her early twenties that she thought she would like to see her birth certificate and to learn from it news of her birth mother.

First, Sarah had to be interviewed by a woman from Social Services. Something she said at that meeting stuck with Sarah: as she handed Sarah the folder, she said, 'You've got to be careful because you could be opening a can of worms; you could be trying to find someone who's awful.'

Her birth mother was Susan George. She'd come from Derbyshire originally, but at the time of Sarah's birth she was twenty-one and had been living in London. The father was Argentinean. Susan met Sarah's father at a club; he was travelling the world, and he left the country before she even knew she was pregnant, so she had no opportunity to tell him. The file detailed all sorts of things Sarah hadn't expected to find out — that Susan George had a good job, what exams she'd passed, that she liked swimming — as well as those she did, like her birth weight and her birth mother's height: 'Five foot four, only a little bit taller than me!'

The social worker who'd overseen the adoption had written that the baby looked like Susan, which Sarah found quite comforting. It was made clear that Susan wanted her baby to have a good family life — a mother and father, and all the right things for her. This was a common theme among many of the women who had been through this awful experience. Young pregnant women were told that adoption would give their baby both a mother and a father and a home full of nice things — things that they themselves would not be able to provide. With little or no support from the state, and often when their own families had refused to offer any help, it was virtually impossible for a young woman with a baby to support herself financially, or even to find herself and her baby somewhere suitable to live. A line at the end stated that Susan expressly wanted the child *not* to go to a Roman Catholic family; Sarah thought that this must be because the Argentinean man had been Catholic and Susan felt strongly about the subject as a result.

The social worker's warning remained with Sarah for quite some time afterwards, so, feeling that she had learned enough, she didn't try to trace Susan George or follow up any of the leads in the file for another few years. She felt no anger towards Susan for her decision, feeling that as a single woman in her very early twenties, she probably had no choice at all. 'I have never judged her, because I knew it was such a different time then. She was away from her family, living in London, with a career, living a brilliant life, or so it seemed. I wouldn't wish for my two girls to be single mothers. If I'd fallen pregnant at that age, I'd have been devastated. It was absolutely the norm to give your baby up for adoption in those circumstances.'

It was having her own children that changed things for Sarah. She hated being reminded of her adopted status when she went to hospital prior to the birth of her children, as she had to fill in forms asking for details of her family's health, and would be forced to put 'don't know' in answer to many of the questions.

Sarah has three children. 'I loved having my children, because it was like they were the only people in the world actually related to me.' This was something she felt everyone else she knew took for granted, but she couldn't, and she realised that she wanted it too. 'It sounds pretty trivial, but it wasn't trivial to me.'

The desire to further that link urged her on. 'My curiosity has always been there, always; it just comes and goes in degrees. I want there to be someone else out there who looks a bit like me, who is a bit like me.'

Sarah revisited the material in the file she had been given, but everything in it was from a long time ago, and almost none of the names and addresses were of any use to her at all. She registered with a number of internet sites, which led nowhere, so in the end she hired a private detective. They went through the records and produced a death certificate for a man who they believed was Sarah's grandfather. On the certificate was the name of Susan's mother — Josephine George. The address was for a village in Derbyshire, a place called Wingerworth, but the street and house name weren't the same as those on Sarah's birth certificate. Sarah looked the village up on a map, but decided against going there — she could see that it wasn't that small and she might be driving around aimlessly for quite a while. Plus she felt she couldn't barge in — suppose her very existence was a secret that few people there knew about?

Once again, Sarah shelved the idea of searching for her birth parent for a few more years. The 'itch' she felt about Susan would come and go, but it never took over, and besides, she took comfort from knowing that her grandmother, Josephine, was in this village and therefore potentially reachable. When she passed women in the street whom she guessed were about Susan's age, Sarah would idly day-dream: 'I wonder if she looks like them? Or if she looks like me?'

It was only when Sarah reached the age of forty that tracing Susan started to become important to her. The thought that she might be too late if she put it off drove her on. However, she decided not to drive to Wingerworth until she could be sure she was going to the right place, and that she would be able to track down Josephine.

Sarah and her husband and children went on holiday to Turkey, where Sarah made friends with a woman, Helene, and they spent their days relaxing by the pool, chatting. The two of them met two other women at the poolside, one of whom let slip that they were both from Wingerworth. Sarah said nothing, but later on she summoned up the courage to speak about her adoption — not something she ever felt she could just blurt out. She said to her new friend, 'Those two women we met earlier today — I want to ask them a question. Do you think I should?' And she went on to explain about her adoption and the link to Wingerworth. 'Why not?' said Helene.

The next day the four of them were beside the pool again. 'I waited for all the kids to go away, and then said, 'Do you mind me asking? I was adopted. My mum was from your village . . . ' and she told them the whole story.

'Wow!' said the women. One of them added, 'I'm going to ring my mum tonight and ask her. What's the address? What's her name?'

At this point Sarah's mind went blank — a name she'd known for years and years just flew out of her head. She rushed over to her husband and asked him. His memory failed him as well. 'No!' Sarah cried. 'We must think! It's a famous actress's name, starts with . . . ' Eventually it came back to her: 'I went rushing over and said to these startled women, 'It's Susan George!''

As it turned out, the two women's families hadn't heard of her, but they told Sarah enough about the place that she felt confident about driving over to see if she could locate the house herself. Again, it wasn't easy for her — she felt she had to dig deep to do this.

Sarah and her husband drove to the village together, to look for the house where Josephine lived. When they got there, Sarah saw a woman in the street and — although she did know the name of the house and the street it was on — thought it might be a good idea to get any other information she could before she knocked on the door. The woman knew Mrs George and which house she'd lived in, but said she'd moved away. She directed Sarah to another house, telling her that the occupier knew Mrs George well and would know where she'd gone to.

Feeling she was edging ever closer to her goal, Sarah went up to the front door and knocked. Several times. Eventually she went down a side passage and knocked at the side door. After what seemed an eternity, an old lady came to the door. Not knowing whether or not anyone in the village knew that Mrs George's daughter had given up a child for adoption, Sarah tried to chat to the woman without having to explain exactly why she needed to know where she had moved to. After a conversation about the garden, Sarah said she was passing through the village and wanted to call on Mrs George. 'I know she's really old. I don't even know if she's alive.'

The old lady at the door retorted, 'Oh, she's not as old as me, dear!' The confirmation that Josephine George was alive — and the sense that she might get some really useful information at long last — kept Sarah riveted, even as she tried to appear as casual as possible, so as not to cause herself any problems.

Sarah pressed on. Where could she reach her? 'She's moved to Sheffield, to a nursing home, to be near her daughter.'

Her heart in her mouth, Sarah said — trying to appear casual as well as knowledgeable — 'Susan?' But the old lady's reply was hard to hear — it sounded like 'Anita, a solicitor'. Before Sarah could press her any further, she added, 'Susan's gone away, either South America or South Africa, I can't remember which.'

Sarah was by now almost fizzing with this new knowledge, but she still had to stay outwardly calm. The old lady then told her that a gentleman who lived next door to Mrs George's old house would know where she was. 'If his car's there, he'll be in.' After thanking her profusely, Sarah rushed round to the other house. The car was there — but after several minutes of knocking, it was clear the man was out. Her search was over.

When they returned home, Sarah wrote to him, saying, 'I came to call on Mrs George today. I spoke to your neighbour (so at least he could check that what Sarah was writing was genuine). Is there any chance you could let me know where Mrs George now lives?' She included a sheet of paper for him to write the address on, her home phone and mobile numbers and a stamped, addressed envelope. She heard nothing from him, which was very disappointing, but, as she said to her husband, 'If someone wrote to you asking where the old lady who lived next door had gone, what would you think?'

Sarah searched through records, but could find nothing about a solicitor called Anita

George, and the list of care homes where Josephine George might be was enormous. It was the last avenue open to her, but it wasn't one she felt she had the strength or the ability to tackle at that time.

Very soon after, Sarah took a call at the gym where she worked as a receptionist. The caller was from a company in London; they were making a programme about reuniting families, about people trying to trace relatives, often after an event such as adoption, and would the gym kindly display a poster so that people could apply? Almost without thinking, Sarah said, 'I want to do that!' If she'd simply seen the poster — or read an advert in the paper — she wouldn't have paid attention to it. She would have assumed that her story wouldn't be of any interest to the *Long Lost Family* team, or, indeed, anyone else. It was the chance moment of answering that phone call that changed things for her. 'I'm that sort of person. My mum used to say to me, 'You let life happen to you; you're not very proactive at all' — and I'm not.'

* * *

One aspect of the process of publicly searching for Susan that deeply troubled

Sarah was the effect it would have on her parents. 'I was risking an awful lot. I was risking my relationship with my parents, whom I have adored all of my life, to do this, and that showed me how strongly I wanted this.' Her mother did not accept that there was any difference between loving an adopted child and loving a biological one. 'If anyone ever suggested it wasn't the same, when I was little, she would say, 'If you had a caesarean and you were given a baby, you'd love that baby the same, even if you didn't know it was the right baby.'' There were even times when it seemed she blanked Sarah being adopted out of her mind. When Sarah's son had a bit of baby eczema, Sarah's mum said to the doctor, 'Oh, he gets that from me,' at which, Sarah gave her a look and her mum rushed out, 'Oh! No, no, sorry, sorry.' Therefore Sarah knew it would be very difficult when she spoke to her mother, and she finished by telling her, 'I wish I wasn't adopted, and I wish you didn't have to go through this, and that I didn't have to go through this.'

Sarah has never felt that being adopted mattered — it didn't define her. So she was appalled when she met a woman who announced — not knowing that Sarah was adopted — 'Oh, we've got four adopted children.' To Sarah, your child is your child, regardless.

Almost every thought about her situation is a conflicting one, and Sarah feels that telling a child they're adopted isn't always the right thing to do. 'Honesty is the best policy — who for? It wasn't better for my mum, learning I wanted to search for Susan. It wasn't better for me, growing up wondering. If I'd never had to think about this, would my life have been better? It's something that forces its way into my mind. It doesn't go away if you don't do anything about it.'

Sarah was instead left wondering. Whether it was on her birthday — 'the one time in the year I hoped she was thinking about me' — or on other occasions, it was the lack of knowledge that worried at her, nagged at her. What did Susan look like? What was she like? What had she done with her life? Had Susan forgotten about her? Suppose she was with somebody who didn't know about Sarah's birth? This immediately set Sarah to thinking, 'If she's anything like me then of course she won't have told anyone.' Having caused upset in her own family, the last thing Sarah wanted was to turn Susan's life upside down 'just for my curiosity'. In her bleakest moments, Sarah would think, 'I've been rejected once — could I take it if she rejected me a second time?'

The *Long Lost Family* team trawled through the Birth, Marriage and Death records, and found that Susan George had become Susan Newall on 7 June 1975, after marrying Alan, but they could find no record of either of them in the UK. Tracing Alan Newall's relatives, they found someone who told them the couple had emigrated to South Africa not long after they were married. As South Africa's electoral rolls were not yet digitised, it was a painstaking process of going through them by hand before they could locate the Newalls. They found Susan just outside Pretoria; she and Alan had a son, twelve years younger than Sarah, but divorced in the 1980s.

When Nicky Campbell met Susan, she was able to tell him some of her story. Working in London, she had met this 'drop-dead gorgeous' man, Alvaro; he asked her to marry him, but Susan thought they were too young. He disappeared from her life, and it was then she discovered she was pregnant.

Susan went to a home for unmarried mothers. There were hundreds of such homes across the country. In 1968, the year Sarah was born, more than 7,000 women went into these homes — and almost all of them gave their children up for adoption. Susan felt she had almost no choice in the matter: 'Being pregnant, and not being married, forty-two years ago, was almost like being branded a witch in the Middle Ages.'

The *Long Lost Family* team were well aware of the sort of experience Susan was talking about, as their research had shown that since those days a shift had taken place in society's attitudes towards single women who became pregnant. 'You cannot imagine the shame of an illegitimate child,' one source had told them. Other women spoke about their experiences in the Mother and Baby Homes, although for some of them their experiences were rather more awful than Susan's. One went to 'a miserable place where the expectant mothers were made to scrub floors on their hands and knees every day', and where — when she was sent for a medical examination — she was made to feel almost as if she was a prostitute. Another remembered the traumatic way in which her baby was removed from her care — her daughter was taken from her cot by the nuns as she slept — and to this day she remained heartbroken at not being allowed to say goodbye. Another remembers sitting watching her child — they weren't allowed to breastfeed them — and hearing a taxi draw up outside. She was told, 'It's time,' and the child was whisked away.

Perhaps the worst moment for Susan came when she had to tell her parents: her father, an ex-Royal Marine Commando, said, 'I didn't expect this of you.' Even the memory of those few words caused Susan to pause in telling her story to Nicky, and sigh deeply.

Once Sarah was born, Susan had to remain with her, looking after her baby for the next five weeks, to make sure she had made the right decision in giving her child up for adoption. Again, the memory of those days — a painful time for Susan — brought her to tears. 'After six weeks, the nurse came and took her away. I'd bought her nice dresses and a teddy, and sent her away with everything. I cried all the way home on the train.'

But Sarah was never far from Susan's thoughts. Not only was everyone fully aware of her existence, Susan had a photograph of baby Sarah on display in her lounge. 'She's never been hidden: my friends know about her, my little church know about her, my son . . . ' When Nicky asked her what she'd done when she'd received the news that Sarah was looking for her, her excitement was understandable. 'I phoned all my friends, my sister in England. I was like a crazy woman. It was very exciting.'

Nicky passed a photograph of Sarah to

Susan, which made her draw in her breath sharply. 'She has my eyes! A beautiful smile.' Asked if she'd ever thought of looking for Sarah, Susan was adamant. 'Who was I to step in and say, 'Well, here I am, I'm your mother, I've come to claim you.' I didn't think that was right. I was afraid of upsetting the apple cart, and especially her adoptive parents.'

Back in the UK, Davina broke the news that Susan had been found. So taken aback that at first she felt she couldn't breathe, Sarah managed to gasp out, 'Have you really?' She was overwhelmed by the news. 'I can't even tell you how thrilled I am. I'm just absolutely speechless.' Davina went on to tell her about Susan's life, and how pleased she was to have heard from Sarah. She showed Sarah Susan's photograph, and handed her a letter. Before she read it, Sarah carried on struggling to get her breath back. 'I am so shocked, absolutely flabbergasted. This is better than anything I could ever have imagined. I can't believe it.'

Dear Sarah Louise,

It was the most wonderful surprise when I received the phone call about you. I was overwhelmed and overjoyed at the thought of being able to meet you at long last. You've been constantly in my thoughts and prayers, and I have a beautiful photo of you as a baby displayed in my lounge. I am longing to meet you and hear all about your life, which I hope has been and is a very happy one.

I was married for eleven years and have a son, Gareth, your brother. He's 31 and married, and has just had twin girls.

I send you lots of love and look forward to seeing you soon.

After all the years of wondering, and all the effort of searching for her, Sarah was jubilant. 'I never thought this was going to happen. I just can't believe that I could be this lucky.' Over the next few days, Sarah re-read the letter again and again. She didn't sleep for days and days, very out of character for her, and she couldn't stop thinking, 'This is amazing!'

Susan flew over from South Africa a fortnight later to meet Sarah.

Before she arrived, Sarah knew that she would have to tell her mother and father that Susan had been found and was now flying over to meet her. They drove down to her parents' house, a journey that, for Sarah, was awful: 'I have never ever felt so sick and bad about having to do something in my life — it was the hardest thing I've ever had to do.'

Sarah's mother and father were totally shocked and heartbroken because it had come out of the blue, and her mother said to Sarah, 'I know this sounds dramatic, but you imagine someone trying to rip one of your children away from you. I don't care if that's not what it's like; that's what it feels like.'

Sarah understands exactly how her mother feels: 'At the end of the day, she's had me from a baby — I'm hers.' But she felt that she needed to meet Susan to understand something about herself. 'I'm hoping I'll find that missing jigsaw piece, the one I've been looking for, for ages. If you've lost something, you're always looking out for it, and now, if I find it, everything will be in its place.'

The reunion

Tuesday, 19 April, 2011. Sarah and Susan were preparing to meet each other. Sarah was determined to make a good impression, and displayed a vulnerability when she said, 'She didn't want to know me once, so I've got to put this best impression forward, so that she'll want to know me this time round.' Susan told Nicky that she was very nervous, and Sarah told Davina exactly the same thing. 'I didn't know I'd feel so scared.

Nobody wants to think someone's disappointed in them.'

When the two of them finally met, any trace of nervousness quickly disappeared. Another aspect of both their personalities came to the fore instead: they both could not believe their luck, and tried to outdo each other in expressing how lucky they thought they were. Susan recognised the link between them immediately, from just a turn of Sarah's head: 'It's like an animal that recognises its young. I knew she was mine.'

Sarah was delighted by so much she heard. When Susan told her she looked just like Susan's mother Josephine, she was thrilled — 'All my life I've wanted to look like someone.'

After the programme

The day after the filming for the programme had finished, Susan went to Sarah's house. She settled herself on the sofa and accepted a cup of tea, but as Sarah's son Sam put it down beside her, Susan stopped him and said, 'Can you get me a spoon, for my sweeteners?' and sat back in astonishment as everyone laughed. Sarah explained that that's the first thing she did whenever she went to someone's home — and that no one else in her family had that trait.

Sarah showed Susan the adoption file she'd received when she was in her twenties. Most of it, Susan couldn't recall at all — she certainly wouldn't have written that she liked swimming, she said, and she would never have insisted that the child shouldn't go to a Roman Catholic family as, being religious herself, she strongly respected all religions.

Sarah met her aunt, Juanita — Josephine had had a love of all things Spanish — which explained why Sarah, hunting for 'Anita', had never managed to track her down. Juanita invited Sarah over to have dinner on the following Saturday, to see Susan again and meet Juanita's daughter, Sarah's cousin, Louise.

The following day Sarah went to work as normal. She hadn't anticipated how she'd feel, and by the end of Thursday she was wailing to a friend, 'Oh God, I can't believe I've got to wait till Saturday to see her again! I've only just met her, I just want to speak to her.'

She says, 'I was completely overreacting — and at that moment, just as I was saying that, Susan texted me. 'So lovely to meet you and I can't wait to see you on Saturday.' I found out later that she couldn't text and this was a very difficult thing for her to do, so that made it even more special. It took me a while to realise what was going on. Meeting her was a bit like falling in love: all I wanted to do for a while was to see her or hear from her.'

At the weekend the two sisters took Sarah to meet their mother Josephine. She was now ninety-four, so it was hard for Sarah to tell if she did look like her, as Susan had claimed, but she enjoyed her company a lot and found her hilarious.

The following week, they travelled down to London to watch the programme that had been made about their meeting. By this point, Sarah was certain they'd talked everything over, but when she saw Susan on screen, talking about how she'd thought about Sarah over all those years, and how she'd taken the news that she was now looking for her, it tipped Sarah over the edge. 'I'm not a big one for crying, but I cried then, and I cried uncontrollably, which is not like me at all. I was drained after watching that.'

They went out for dinner. Susan was telling Sarah about the time she lived in London before Sarah was born, and talked, in passing, about an episode from those times, 'when I was pregnant with you', and Sarah thought, 'I've never had anyone say those words to me before.'

A couple of days later Susan flew back to South Africa. Her son, Gareth, texted Sarah to say she'd arrived and that she was really upset, 'but we've got her under control'. Another family resemblance made itself known to Sarah then — Gareth communicated with his 'new' sister in the same way Sarah herself did, sounding very excited: 'I'm so excited, Big Sis. It's going to be amazing.' Sarah felt an affinity with him already. Of course he'd grown up knowing about her, and his enthusiasm was born in part out of that knowledge. 'I used to say when I was young that I wished I had a sister,' Sarah says. 'Now I'm really glad that I haven't, because then there would already be someone in that daughter role.'

Once Susan had gone back to South Africa, Sarah's life returned to its previous state. For a while, her need to hear from and speak to Susan was at the fore, but gradually her children's needs returned to centre stage, and Sarah returned to her former busy existence. The whole experience, where everything ran to such a tight schedule, had heightened their emotions. If Susan had been living in Derbyshire, it might have been less intense.

An unexpected aspect of being involved in the programme were the people — strangers

— who came up and spoke to her after recognising her from the TV. Among them were a number of people who wanted to talk about their own adoption stories. Sarah became more formally involved in this when she spoke to prospective adoptive parents for her local Social Services. 'When you adopt a child now, you have to go on a course. They had completed the other aspects of the course, and I was brought in on the last evening, to give them the opportunity to ask me questions.' It was only thanks to the *Long Lost Family* programme that Sarah was able to do this. The twenty or so people on the course had drafted a list of questions and — after giving Sarah ten minutes to read through them — they then asked her to talk about the issues they'd raised, along with anything she wanted to add. Luckily for her, 'There was nothing they couldn't have asked me that I hadn't already been asked, so that made it really easy.'

Sarah's relationship with her adoptive parents is something she thinks about all the time. She has no hesitation in thinking of them as 'Mum and Dad'; that has never wavered. It was hard for her to explain why she felt she had to go through the process of searching for Susan, but she tried to do that. The one thing she would like to be able to do is to talk about both sides of her family without anyone feeling threatened. She was planning to fly out to see Susan in South Africa, and her mother and father were emotional about the news when Sarah told them. Sarah's problem is that the person she relies upon most — the person she would turn to, to ask for advice in how to handle such a tricky situation — is precisely the person she can't ask. The fact that she has upset her mother is, for Sarah, the downside of finding and meeting Susan.

Watching the programme made Sarah's mum realise just how much she loved her, more than she realised, just as you would expect if you think you're going to lose someone close to you. 'I told her in phone calls over the following weeks that she can't and won't lose me. I can't tell her Susan's not important to me, because that's not true — she is very important.' It's a very hard path for Sarah to negotiate, and she's not through it yet.

9

Wendy and Sharon, Two Sisters Searching

You don't know what to do. You don't know whether to grieve. It's very, very hard.

The search for Sarah Wade, someone who vanished without a trace when she was in her early twenties, was a potentially difficult one for the *Long Lost Family* team to take on, because people who go missing often want to stay missing. As a young woman, with no ties, Sarah could have travelled to live almost anywhere in the world, and it was possible that she had gone missing deliberately — because she no longer sought contact of any sort with her family. Until they could track Sarah Wade down, no one could be certain whether or not she would want to be reunited with her brothers and sisters. This had the potential to be the most traumatic case the team handled throughout the series.

Sarah's disappearance from their lives cast a long shadow over a family that was a happy one, even though they had all been through a difficult time. While her two brothers and three sisters were all united in their concern for Sarah's well-being, it was the two middle sisters, Sharon and Wendy, who approached *Long Lost Family*. The two of them voiced the questions that all the family wanted answered about what had happened to their younger sister.

Wendy said, 'I just need to know she's okay, or not okay. I feel that I've come to the point where I just need to know.'

Sharon added, 'We don't know whether she's alive or not. We just don't know.'

Sarah's absence has forced them to do more than search for her — it's also made them consider why she left their lives in the first place: 'In the back of your mind, you just keep asking, why?' said Sharon. Questions like this had come to dominate their lives.

The family had all lived in Croydon. When Sharon was seven and Wendy four, their mother — divorced from their father — met and married Jim. He was very much their dad as they were growing up; although they called him Jim, they always referred to him as their dad if they were explaining who he was to someone. The reason for this confusion was because Jim was black, and his wife and all her children were white.

Until, that is, Sarah was born, five years later. 'When Sarah was born,' said Sharon, 'it was a complete family.' They would all help their mum look after Sarah, and they lavished attention on her. 'It changed our lives when she was born. We had a little sister that we all doted on,' said Wendy.

Sharon and Wendy's most vivid memories of Sarah are as a young girl on the beach at Selsey on the south coast, where the family always holidayed. Sarah would be noticed by others on the beach, according to Wendy and Sharon, thanks to her addictive laugh. She would have so much fun that, 'Everybody was looking at her enjoying herself in the water,' said Sharon.

Wendy added, 'Whether it was there or at home, she was always the centre of it all.' Sarah's good nature and obvious happiness was something the whole family took pleasure in. Throughout her childhood and teenage years, she remained the centre of her family's life, her natural ebullience never troubled, or so it seemed to Sharon; 'If she was ever down, she never showed it.'

As Sarah grew up, her older brothers and sisters moved out of the family home, but she continued to be the focus of their attention. When Wendy was married, Jim walked her down the aisle. When she had children, Sarah was a brilliant auntie to them — she was only eight years older than Wendy's eldest — and she was as bubbly and extrovert a young woman as she had been as a young girl.

But when Sarah was twenty-two, in 1997, their mother was diagnosed with cancer. Sarah was by then the only one of the children still living at home. This meant that despite everything the rest of her family would do for their parents, Sarah was always the one there at the beginning and end of every day. That their mother was so ill was something of a turnaround for the family, as it was usually Jim (who was partially sighted) who complained of feeling unwell. Sarah coped with them both. 'She had so much responsibility; she was the one there when we all went home,' said Wendy. 'When Mum was ill, Sarah was looking after her through the night, things like that. I think that for her, at that time, it must have been incredibly hard.'

A mere three months after her diagnosis, and at the age of only fifty-eight, Sarah's mum died. Tragically, within a year, at the age of seventy-four, and again almost without any warning, Jim also passed away. This was even more shocking to them all. Wendy observed, 'During all of that, I only saw Sarah break down a few times. I think she was very good at hiding what she was feeling. And she was probably protecting us as well.'

The deaths of both of their parents so soon

after each other was an awful time for the whole family, and had a massive impact not just on all of the children, but on their children too — the pair of them had been, in Wendy's words, 'ideal grandparents'. However, as Sarah was the only one living at home, she was the most affected by these traumatic events. She had an older boyfriend, Joe, with whom she spent increasing amounts of time in the aftermath of her parents' deaths, and she saw her family less and less.

Within three months of the deaths of their parents, the council took back the family home, where they had lived since their marriage. For Sarah, this meant she had not only lost her mother and father, but also the only home she'd ever known. She continued to present a brave face to her family as the place was gradually cleared, till the day came when she had to move out. 'It was awful, it was just an empty shell, and everything had gone,' said Wendy, 'but it was like she was portraying she was happy, she was going to be fine, she was with her boyfriend and they were going to be okay.'

Sarah told her sisters and brothers that she was going to move up to north London, to Joe's flat. She didn't pass on a landline number, but she took with her their mother's mobile, so they could contact her on that. She was also in touch with Wendy's son on MSN Messenger. When they were younger, before texting had become ubiquitous, she and Wendy's son had shared a computer and used to use MSN regularly.

Sarah would still make the occasional trip down to see them, and Wendy recalled that she became concerned about her younger sister after one visit. Sarah appeared not to be looking after herself properly, which Wendy was horrified by, and she wondered to herself, 'What would Mum think?' Wendy took Sarah out shopping in Croydon, to buy her some clothes and a new coat. At the end of the day, Sarah got back on the train and headed back to north London.

The messages on MSN dropped away. The mobile phone account was stopped. The family contacted some of Sarah's friends in the Croydon area, to see if they had had any news of her, but they too hadn't heard from Sarah and couldn't make contact. No one seemed to know where she was. One of her brothers, together with his brother-in-law, went to the address they'd been given in north London to see if they could find out what had happened to Sarah, but they couldn't make any contact at all with her. She had vanished from their lives.

The family didn't see her again for nearly thirteen years.

There wasn't a day that went by during those years when one or other of the siblings, or Sarah's nieces and nephews, wouldn't think to themselves, 'Where is Sarah? What is she up to? I hope she's alright.' Whenever there was any family occasion or gathering of any sort, someone would say that Sarah was the only thing that seemed to be missing from the group. None of them felt any anger towards Sarah at all, and they understood that as more time went by it would become more and more difficult for her to get back in touch with them. They desperately hoped that this was the only reason Sarah hadn't contacted them. They became desperate to find her. Even if they couldn't see her, they all wanted to know that she was okay and happy — that was the overriding thing for them all.

Sharon worried that things might have gone drastically wrong for Sarah: 'I hope she's not living on the streets, or is in a bad way.' Wendy had by now started working as a social worker, and through her training became only too aware of some of the things that can happen to someone separated from their family, vulnerable and isolated. 'People can go off the rails and never come back from that.' She tried not to think about this, but she was realistic about what might have happened to Sarah. She couldn't think of any reason Sarah might have wanted to distance herself from her family, other than the fact that she had been through a traumatic time, and that she'd not opened up to her family about her feelings then.

Over a dozen years, the family tried everything they could think of to find her, even turning to specialists who trace missing persons. Wendy wrote a letter to Sarah that the Missing Persons Bureau took, hoping to track Sarah down and pass it to her, so that she'd know they hadn't forgotten her.

Despite this, Sarah remained missing. Fearing the worst, the family seized on any news that might lead to her. Sharon heard a rumour, from old friends of Sarah's boyfriend Joe, that he might have moved to the south coast. 'We heard rumours that she was in Brighton. We went looking everywhere for her: the seafront, the backstreets, the pier, everywhere. Nothing came of it.'

The family were unable to think of any other approach they could take until they found out about *Long Lost Family*. Sharon explained their sense of desperation: 'When you lose somebody, you grieve and you know they're gone. But with Sarah, we didn't know where she was, and it was very hard.'

Taking on a missing persons case is tricky. The worst fear was that she'd died. So the first thing that had to be done was to check the death records — and it was with a sense of relief that no name came up. Once that was out of the way, the research team started back at the beginning. Sarah had last been known to be living in north London; so they began by looking through the electoral rolls there, to eliminate that possibility, before they moved on to deal with the idea, thought to be no more than a rumour, that she was on the south coast somewhere.

The team found that there were over twenty Sarah Wades or S. Wades living in the Greater London area. However, one stood out. There was an S. Wade living at the same north London address the family had visited all those years ago. Nicky Campbell said, 'It seemed extraordinary that Sarah could have been hiding from her family for all these years, living at her last known address. We wrote her a letter and she replied, confirming she was the woman we were looking for.' She did agree to meet Nicky, who wondered, 'What could have made her hide for so long? Is the fact that she's willing to talk a sign that she's willing to reunite with her family?'

When Sarah's parents had died so

suddenly and so close together, and then when her home was taken away from her when what she needed most in the world was stability, she'd felt lost. She tried to pretend to her family that she was dealing with it, but the happy entertainer who made everyone smile was long gone — on the inside, she had never felt so low. It was, to her, as if a bomb had been dropped on their family and had ripped their world apart.

Sarah told Nicky, 'The rocky time started when my mum was diagnosed with cancer, and they gave her a couple of months to live. She died three months later. That was very difficult. Just about a year later, my dad died, very suddenly. That was the catalyst that exploded everything, the way I saw it. After that, nothing was right.'

Overwhelmed by grief, Sarah decided that, with no home left there for her, being near her brothers and sisters in the Croydon area made things more painful for her. She thought that by putting a bit of distance between them, things would become easier; it wasn't meant to be anything other than her stepping back from an awful time in her life. 'For me, at the time, I didn't think of it as running away. I just thought of it as taking some time out, and just getting myself together, gathering myself, really.'

She didn't want to worry them with her grief, and didn't have the strength to maintain the happy exterior they all expected of her. So she moved in with her boyfriend Joe, who lived in north London. 'It was only ever meant to be short-term. I never meant to lose contact with my family; that was never part of the plan.'

Sarah sank into a deep, deep depression. Weeping at the memory of the pain of it all, she told Nicky that it was 'very, very bad'. She wanted to maintain contact with her family: 'I needed to speak to them, and I needed to see them, but I . . . couldn't bring myself to do it. I couldn't bring myself to let them see or hear me being that depressed.' And after months of silence, how could she go back to them? Why hadn't they tried to find her? Perhaps they were angry? She didn't have the strength to face them, and was scared of their disappointment, so despite needing their support more than ever, she stayed silent and the months turned into years.

Nicky asked, 'Did you not think about picking up a phone?'

Sarah replied that she was fearful of being rejected. 'I was worried that they would just say, 'D'you know what, Sarah? You've left it so long, we don't know who you were. We're not really interested anymore.' That was my ultimate fear.'

Nicky reassured her that this was very far from being the case. He asked Sarah if she remembered receiving a letter from Wendy via the Missing Persons Bureau. Sarah did remember it. 'I got a letter, saying that Wendy was trying to find me, was looking for me, and at that point, I went into panic mode. I just went into shut-down mode. I thought it could only be something bad, and I didn't want to hear any bad news. I wasn't ready at the time. I don't think I was ready to speak to them, to see them.'

* * *

Sarah never intended to stay away this long. She had only recently come out of the depression that had plagued her for the best part of a decade. She missed Wendy, Sharon and the rest of her family more than she could describe, and was desperate to see them again. She wanted to tell them how sorry she was to have made them worry. She'd thought of them every day since she'd last seen them — she just wanted her family back.

Nicky had brought with him another letter, which Wendy had written on behalf of all of the family. Before he gave it to her, he asked Sarah what she felt when she heard that her family were looking for her. 'Well, I was surprised, very surprised.' Thinking about the amount of time that had passed since she'd last seen them set her off crying, and the letter only added to this.

Sarah,

How can I start a letter to you, I have asked myself. I want you to know how many memories I have of my little sister Sarah, that go through my mind most days. It really has been awful not having you around. I always go back to our happy memories, when you always made us laugh and we would laugh at silly things. I also wonder why you have not been in contact, what made you stay away? I most of all hope you're happy, your life is happy, and you're being looked after and loved. I have never given up on finding you, Sarah.

Love you always, Wendy

Sarah said, 'That's lovely. I think it might be okay. It's going to be okay, I think. I really want to see them now. So much.'

Nicky told Sarah that there hadn't been a day they hadn't thought about her. 'There hasn't been a day I haven't thought about them,' she replied.

When Davina McCall went to give Sharon and Wendy the amazing news — that Sarah had been found, living where they thought she might once have been — they burst into tears of relief. While they were both shocked that she was found where she was — and Wendy was immediately cross with herself for not going there more often — they were also delighted beyond words that she was alive and well. 'That's amazing, the best thing.'

Davina explained to them what had happened during those missing years: 'I can only offer you my take on what she's been through. She's been completely traumatised by grief, shut herself down, and she just withdrew. When she started feeling a bit better, it was a long time later, and she felt, 'I've missed too many occasions, too many birthdays. What if they are angry or annoyed with me?' '

Sharon rushed to point out that they were never angry with her. At which point Davina produced a photograph of Sarah to show them both. 'Oh, she hasn't changed a bit,' they immediately agreed. And then it was their turn to read and weep over a letter.

Dearest Wendy and Sharon,

I am so happy to be writing this to you both. I've often wondered if this would ever happen, our getting in contact again, but as I write this, I am happy. It was never supposed to be like this, my moving 'north of the river' was never meant to herald over a decade of silence, but as the days turned to weeks and then months and eventually years, I suppose I thought you'd all be better off without me around. [At this point, the two sisters said, 'Never!' and 'Why would she think that?']

I don't know where that idea came from, but it was there, and I listened to it and stayed away from everyone. I miss you all so much that not a day goes by that I'm not thinking of you. I'm so sorry I've hurt you in the process. Thank you for not giving up on me. I love you so much. Can't wait to see you!

Your smelly sister, Sarah

The verdict was that the prospect of being reunited with their sister was, 'So lovely. I feel complete, and that all the wondering is finally over.'

The reunion

The three of them arranged to meet on the beach at Selsey. This was to be the first time Sarah went back there since she went missing. She was really excited now by the prospect of meeting up with her family again, 'Now we're here, I can't wait.' Just being by the seaside brought loads of good memories flooding back for her. 'This is as I remember it. This is great.' The positive feeling lifted her, and it enabled her to feel ready to greet her family. 'I'm just really excited to see my sisters again now. I just want to give them a big hug and find out how they're doing.'

Sharon acknowledged that the prospect of reuniting with her long-lost sister was making her feel very tense and upset. As soon as the three of them caught sight of each other, they rushed into each other's arms and sobbed. 'Let me look at your face,' said Wendy, so overcome to be seeing her sister again after all these years.

'You've never ever been out of our minds,' Sharon reassured her. 'Never ever.'

Throughout the next few minutes, Wendy and Sharon gripped Sarah's hands as if they were determined never to let her go again. All three of them were euphoric, but at the same time Sarah wanted to tell them something. With effort, she said, 'I just want to say to you both, I'm sorry that I just disappeared. It was never meant to be like that.'

Wendy pointed out that, 'We all had to deal with Mum and Dad dying in our own way. The one thing that's been missing is you. I don't want anything else now we've got you back.'

Sarah said to them both, 'These last few weeks, all I've wanted to do is see you. I missed you so much. I just think I'm going to be okay.'

Sharon stroked her younger sister's face and comforted her. 'We're here now, we're not going anywhere.'

Then, to relive their childhood memories, the three of them took off their shoes and went down to the water's edge to paddle in the sea.

After the programme

All of her brothers and sisters, and their children too, were delighted to be reunited with Sarah. Since the programme, they have all been in regular contact with her, and she has been to parties and outings with them all.

Wendy observed, seeing her sister again, that, 'Sarah has a strong streak in her. Once she got that back, she could cope with us. She had to be in the right place to come back into all our lives.' Her return to her family has been completely natural for all of them: 'It feels like she's just walked back through the door, like it was yesterday she went away,' said Wendy.

What with the Royal Wedding party they threw, a trip on the Thames for Wendy's son's birthday and a visit to the London Aquarium with her niece, Sarah is fully reunited with her brothers and sisters. She comes down and stays with them, and is her old self with them all, although she does have to remind them she has grown up — 'I can get a train home on my own, you know!'

She has discussed her depression with them, and how it dogged her for so long. Wendy pointed out that time slipped away from all of them, as they were all busy in their lives. It was what happened, that's all. In talking about it, and on the TV programme too, Wendy hopes that the issue will become one people can talk about openly. She doesn't want anyone to think that it is some sort of deep, dark secret that needs to be concealed.

Since the programme, she has met a number of people who have talked to her about their own need to look for people missing from their lives. Wendy offers them the experience her family had, in the hope that it'll help, and is happy to tell them all how the whole family is thrilled to have Sarah back with them at last.

10

Carole, Who Has a Brother and Sisters to Locate

'Because my dad wasn't there, I felt angry, and thought I must have done something wrong, and I didn't know what. He said he'd come back and buy me a puppy . . . I never saw him again.'

Carole Davies, who has recently retired, has lived in Wales all her life. Married to Des, her family means everything to her. Between the two of them, they have seven children, eighteen grandchildren and six great-grandchildren. She herself, though, grew up without her father, and as an only child. 'I didn't have any brothers and sisters. I didn't have a father figure. There was my mum, my gran, and that was it.' For Carole, though, there is a whole side of her family that she's never known.

When Carole's mother, Miriam, and father, Gerald, married, the two of them moved in with his father and mother. Carole's father was in the Royal Navy, and the Second World War was in its final year. 'I was a war baby, I suppose,' Carole said, as she was born on 28 January 1946.

The family continued to live with Gerald's parents until Carole was about six months old. Then her parents split up, and Carole and her mother went to live with her maternal grandmother, and that's where Carole remained until she was married at the age of twenty. 'Growing up without my dad was quite a lonely time. Everybody else seemed to have a dad. That was quite upsetting because I felt as if I was missing out on an awful lot.'

Whatever the rights and wrongs of the breakdown of the marriage, it was clear that the couple couldn't live together anymore. 'I don't really know an awful lot about what happened with my parents. I know that it wasn't a very happy marriage, and my mum didn't talk about him an awful lot.' As her mother never told her what had gone on between the two of them, Carole had to rely on what her grandmother said about the marriage — and it's not surprising that she took her daughter's side. 'From what I gathered from my grandmother, he was cruel to my mum. I suppose that's why they got divorced.'

At the end of the war, divorce rates — which had been low during the fighting, with just over 800 divorces recorded in England and Wales in 1941 — rose dramatically. In 1947 there were over 60,000 petitions for divorce. However, divorce still carried a huge stigma, and the whole experience had clearly traumatised Carole's mother. When Carole did ask questions of her mother, she felt they were brushed aside, as if the subject was still taboo. 'The only specific thing I can remember my mum talking about was that they'd lived with his mother and father, and that it was not a very good time. I think his parents interfered in the marriage a lot, and it was quite upsetting for them. My mum was a bit anti-men in the end; I think because it was such a bad marriage. She never bothered with anybody again. I was very curious, I wanted to know an awful lot about him, but because I loved my mum and respected her so much, I didn't want to hurt her feelings, so I kept it inside.'

The distance Carole's mother Miriam kept from her ex-husband extended also to her in-laws. 'I can remember going to my father's parents' house only twice,' recalled Carole, 'and when we did go there, they never spoke about my father.' All Carole knew of her father was that he was in the Royal Navy when her parents married, in the submarine branch. When the war was over, Gerald stayed in the navy for another nine years.

He eventually remarried, and the address of the house in Ropers Avenue in Chingford, Essex, where he moved with his new wife was imprinted on Carole's brain, after she was told it by her mother. As far as she knows, he never had any contact with her mother after that. Miriam, meanwhile, tried to fill the role of both parents, but although she tried hard, Carole was still very conscious of a gap in her life. When her friends talked about their home life, Carole felt left out. 'When they talked about their mums and dads, I couldn't say anything about my dad at all. It was quite hard. I felt I missed out on quite a lot because my dad wasn't there. Why wasn't he? I felt angry that he wasn't there. I felt he could have got in touch with me, even if my mum didn't want to get in contact with him. He could have written to me, sent me birthday cards, that sort of thing. But he never did. So I felt angry towards him about that.'

One issue between her parents that she was aware of was money; it was always in short supply. Her mother worked in a factory, nine to five, every day. 'She found that very hard,' remembers Carole, but what made her feel 'a bit bitter as well' was the issue of maintenance. 'I don't think my mum got much maintenance from him, so she worked really hard. I didn't understand a lot about that because, of course, I was so young.'

'I can remember going back and forth to solicitors when I was little, when my mum was trying to get maintenance. She never seemed to be able to. I think he sent some money now and again at first, and then he didn't, and that was going on for an awfully long time. I felt that he didn't care enough about me to want to help my mum, and I did feel hurt.' Carole's childhood was happy though, and she doesn't remember issues like that hanging heavily over the family. 'When you're young, you don't think about those things for any length of time.'

That her father had remarried was all Carole knew about him until one day, when Carole was fourteen, her mother made a surprise announcement which made it clear that she did have at least some contact with Gerald. 'She said to me, 'Oh, your dad's coming today, he wants to take you out.' I was so excited.' Carole's mother had been shopping and had bought her a new skirt and blouse to wear for the occasion. 'I was over the moon. I thought I was going to look very smart. It was going to be really fun.'

Carole's mum decided that she was going to keep well out of the way when her ex-husband came to the house, so Carole's grandmother went to the door with her when he arrived. 'There was this man standing there, alongside a tallish, fair-haired woman and two small children.' Carole remembers becoming 'really quite shy' because, of course, she didn't know her father at all — and he didn't know her. Their opening lines to each other were quite stilted. 'I'm your dad,' he told her.

'I said, 'Yes, I know.'' The awkwardness of the situation continued. 'It was a bit sort of, 'Hello, this is my wife, these are my children' — at that time I didn't know their names. And he said, 'Can I take you out?' I said yes, and we went more or less straight away; none of them came into the house.

'I didn't know he had any children until that day, when I found out I had a brother and sister. No one had said anything to me about it.'

There was something else that no one spoke about. 'I was only fourteen and had no experience of such things, but I thought that his wife looked as if she might be pregnant, unless she was a bit plump.' The two children were called Keith and Lynne, and they were five and three years old respectively.

The group went in Gerald Thomas's car to Roath Park in Cardiff, and went rowing out on the boating lake there. Carole remembers it vividly as a special and wonderful day. 'My dad and his wife — I can't even remember anyone telling me her name — were making a big effort with me. We went in the rowing boat, and we were all rowing together. It was lovely. We spent a long time on the lake and in the park itself — had lunch there and stayed for the day. It was a very bright, sunny day, and we all enjoyed ourselves an awful lot.'

Apart from spending time with her father, one of the aspects of the day that was so special to Carole was meeting her brother and sister. As an only child, living with her mother and grandmother, Carole never felt she had enough company of her own age. 'I grew up not having any connection with children except for my school friends. My house was more or less all grown-up women, with no children involved in my growing-up years.' She remembers clearly thinking, 'I've got a brother and sister now. I'm not just an only child. I was thrilled to bits.'

At the end of a day that Carole had enjoyed so much, her father drove her back to her grandmother's home. As he dropped her off at her front door, he said, 'Would you like a puppy?'

Carole replied, 'Oh, I'd love one.'

She had never had a pet of her own as, with

her mum working during the day while Carole was at school, there was nobody at home to care for one. Carole was excited, and so she asked her grandmother straight away whether she would help Carole with the puppy, and her grandmother said, 'Yes, if you want it,' and she was able to accept her father's offer. He said, 'Okay, in a few days' time, I'll come back and I'll bring the puppy.' He had already told Carole that after a few days in Wales, he was returning to London.

'And that was it. I thought he would call back in a couple of days' time with the puppy, spend an hour with me and then go back to his home in London. And I waited and waited and waited, and there was no sign of him, no puppy, no nothing. I wouldn't have minded not getting the puppy, as long as he'd come to say goodbye. But he didn't. He just left, and I didn't hear from him, ever, from that day onward.'

Carole's father never came back, with or without a puppy, or made contact with her again. That day was the first and last time she ever saw her brother and sister. 'I was upset for a long time afterwards. I was very angry, and thought I must have done something wrong, and I didn't know what. I felt cheated, I felt hurt, because I'd had an insight into my brother and sister, and then all of a sudden it was taken away from me, gone. It was terrible.'

'I felt cheated. It was like giving a present to somebody at Christmas and then, all of a sudden, taking it away from them. I would have preferred not to have met my brother and sister at all than to have met them and then had them taken away like that. At the time, I thought I would be spending time with them on a regular basis, that we would be connected. But nothing happened after that.'

Carole never saw her father again. 'That is the only memory I have of my father because that's the only time I saw him. So it's something that I think about a lot. I remember the day so well because it is the only memory I have of him. It's something I treasure.'

* * *

Carole felt her father might not be a nice man, in part because of what she'd been told, but also now because of her own experience of dealing with him: 'At fourteen you think your dad's going to be there to help you.'

But as she grew from a teenager into a woman, and even more so after she was married and had her own children, her views changed. 'As you grow older, you realise that there are two sides to every story. Maybe he'd wanted to have a lot more to do with me, but perhaps my mum didn't want him to. Maybe there was something like that going on, I don't know.'

Without anything to go on other than her own speculation, Carole tried to put herself in her mother's shoes, to understand her perspective as a single mother in this situation. 'I often thought that perhaps my mother prevented him from being involved with me because she was worried he wanted to take me. I was the only child, and my mother was very possessive and protective of me, and perhaps she was worried about that aspect of it. Perhaps she was worried that my father would want to take me away from her.'

The lack of information about her own early years and the relationship between her parents frustrated Carole. 'Perhaps my mum didn't want him to stay in contact with me — or maybe he didn't want to. I don't know. This is why I'm so curious to find out the reason why he didn't come to visit me again. Whether there was a reason my mum didn't want him to come. It's just very confusing.' Carole said she thought of every possibility as an explanation as to what happened, and over the years it bothered her as often as she'd allow it to.

At the time, however, Carole reacted in the way that children do. While on the one hand she was angry with her father for not keeping his promise to her and not staying in touch, she also wondered if she had done something that had put him off. 'When he didn't visit me again, I felt angry towards him, and I blamed him for all of it. But I also felt that perhaps I'd done something wrong, something that he didn't like.' She knows now that this is not likely, but that is how she thought as a child — even down to wondering if she had been the cause of their break-up. 'It's just that you think all sorts of things when you're growing up, that maybe it was your fault that they broke up. Well, it's obvious to me now that this wasn't the case, because I was only six months old, so it must have been something between my parents that went on that I didn't know of.

'All through my life I thought about my father, and worried about why he didn't want to bother with me. I always wanted to know what he looked like, because I wanted to know whether I looked like him or my mum.'

Carole has only one photograph of her father, taken on her parents' wedding day, of them both in a garden. He is in his uniform, and her mother carries a bouquet. Carole cherished this picture, as it was the only thing she had with any link to him. However, it just wasn't enough for her to go on: 'I couldn't remember whether he was a handsome man, whether he had scars or anything. Nothing at all.' As Carole grew older, her father stayed the same age in her mind; forever a young man, smiling in the sunshine with his bride, fixed in time in his naval uniform. 'I'd have liked to have some photographs of him as he was growing old, because to me he was always a twenty-year-old.'

When Carole's mother died, in 1998, she felt at liberty to look for her father, now that she knew there was no one to be upset by her search for the missing portion of her family. 'As you grow older, you want to know about your past. It seemed to be an obsession with me, to try to find out about them.' With the help of friends and family, she looked up her father's address, as she had remembered it for all those years, and searched for him on the internet. Unfortunately, she drew a blank, and continued to draw a blank for some years.

In 2008, she did manage to track her father down, but sadly she learned that he had died in 2002. 'I felt so gutted that I'd left it so late to try and delve into it. I wish that I'd started all this a lot earlier, so that I could have met him again. That would have been amazing. But it wasn't to be, which is a shame — a very great shame. I felt very upset. I had a little bit of a cry, but I can't really say that I grieved for him, because there was nothing there — I didn't know him. So I couldn't really do any more than have a little weep and think, 'What an awful shame that I didn't do it a lot earlier.' It would have been amazing if we could have met up. And obviously that will never happen now.'

With only her imagination to help her, Carole has speculated about what her father must have been like. 'I'd like to think he was a nice person. I'm sure he was, because he was married a second time and had two children, and obviously they stayed together. I just wonder why he, as a father to two other children, could not be a father to me in some way as well. I'd just like to think that he did think of me sometimes.'

Almost as soon as Carole learned about her father's death, her thoughts turned to searching for her brother and sister. 'I have a wall of photos at home, but it's missing some.' She would like to have photographs of the brother and sister she met all those years ago — she has never forgotten them. With her father's death, the link to her siblings was even more important to her. 'Because of my father dying, the drive to find out about my brother and sister was uppermost in my mind, to find them and get to know them. If I didn't find them, I wouldn't find anything out about my father at all. There were fifty years of his life that I wanted to know about. I wanted to know my siblings, and maybe try to make up for lost time.'

However, Carole's search for them proved fruitless. 'I tried everything to find my brother and sister. I thought it would be quite an easy thing to find people on the internet, and I felt devastated really that I couldn't get any further than I had.'

Carole's whole family knew the story of her missing brother and sister, and were all very supportive of her search. 'I think they heard about it until they were sick of it really,' Carole laughed. 'It was something I kept going on about, but they understood. They were very much behind me, so I knew that if it came off, it would be a very big thing for them as well, because then they'd see me happy.'

For Carole, having a brother and sister who were part of her life would mean so much. At the time, she said, 'I would have my family, a brother and sister and nephews and nieces. And I've never been able to say that. I'd like to think that I look like one of them, or maybe they look like my dad. To put faces to the names, to be able to say, 'That's my brother and my sister' would be absolutely amazing. It'd be like winning the lottery, because they're my blood relations.'

Carole wondered where her brother and sister might be, and what they did. 'I thought they might still be near where my father lived. I'd always thought of them as being in London. I wondered what sort of work they did, if they had children, what their children did. I didn't care whether they had important jobs or didn't work at all — I just wanted to know.'

After so many years of unsuccessfully searching for her siblings, Carole was understandably nervous about contacting them, if they could be located. She had no idea if they would be interested in being in touch with her, as she did not know what they had been told about her, or if they had been told about her at all. 'I felt that they might not want to meet me. I would have been very upset over that. It would have been quite gut-wrenching, if that was the case.' She was concerned about this because she couldn't help wondering why they hadn't made any attempt to find her over the years, at least as far as she knew. Worse still was the prospect of not finding them at all.

Her search seems to have become something of an obsession with her, and — just as when she was younger and would think about her father and why he wasn't involved in her life — she wondered sometimes why she didn't know her siblings. 'I often spoke to my husband about this, asked his opinion. I said, 'How will I feel if they don't want to meet me and get involved with me?' He replied, 'Well, it wouldn't be because of you as a person. The only reason they wouldn't want to get in contact with you would be that they might feel that it was disrespectful to the memory of their father, because he never contacted you himself.' I thought that, yes, that might be the reason. I worried about the possibility that they might not want to know me, because being rejected would obviously hurt, but I'd have to understand that.'

Carole explained why she had made contact with the programme-makers. 'I want to know more now, because I'm going to be sixty-five. When you're getting older, you think more about your past, and you want to know a little bit more about your own family. I want to know my past. I want to know what happened.

Carole wasn't able to give the *Long Lost Family* team much to assist them in their search. 'I don't know an awful lot about my brother and sister. All I know is that their names are Keith and Lynne. Obviously, Keith's surname is Thomas, but if Lynne's married, her name is going to be different. And that's all I know.' Beyond that, it was a mystery.

Ironically, the one thing the team had going for them in this case was the fact that the man at the very heart of it, Carole's father, had died, which meant there would be a death certificate. The researchers ordered Gerald Thomas's death certificate, as such documents can provide a wealth of information to the trained eye, and they hoped there would be something there that would lead them to his children.

The most obvious thing to check on first was the address where Gerald had been living when he died, as a member of the family could possibly still be living in the family home. But when they wrote to the address, no one had heard of the Thomas family. The next item to check on the certificate was the name of the person who had recorded the death — in this case, an Olwen Christine Camfield, who was listed as Gerald Thomas's daughter. Olwen was obviously a half-sister that Carole knew nothing about. Now the team were looking for three people, not just two. Running traces on Olwen, Lynne and Keith led only to blanks for Olwen and Lynne, but not so with Keith — he was located. Through him, the three siblings were told their sister Carole was searching for them.

Davina went to meet with the three of them, and to find out from them what they knew about Carole — and whether or not they wanted to meet her.

Ollie, the eldest of the three, knew from an early age that her father had a daughter from a previous marriage. 'I can remember a time when I was quite small, probably four or five, posting a letter, and this was a letter that went to Cardiff, and it went every week, and in it was a postal order. Inquisitive child that I was, I managed to get out of Mum that this was a maintenance postal order for my dad's first wife and his daughter.'

While Ollie remembered looking forward to putting the envelope into the post box, she also recalled that her parents often argued about money. Sometimes, when money was really tight, the weekly maintenance would come out of her account — always to be put back. 'I seem to have always known her name was Carole. But I knew I had to keep it a secret. I don't know why, it seemed the natural thing to do, and I didn't tell anybody.'

Shortly after the time Ollie was old enough to understand what was going in the envelopes, and what it meant, the maintenance payments would have come to an end anyway. In those days, once Carole reached her mid-teens, she would have been considered old enough to work, and her father would have stopped paying for her keep. Ollie regrets that she never discussed this with her father, so she thinks she can only have learned this from her mother.

When Keith was five years old and Lynne three, their father took them for a day out with a young girl. They were never told this girl was their sister Carole. They have vague memories of the day — they remember being with a girl and going to the park and then on a boat ride. Keith doesn't know where the lake was — his most vivid memory from that day was when his father pointed up to a row of houses and told him that 'that's where Shirley Bassey used to live'. He knows there was another girl with them, and later on he realised that she would have been Carole, but he can't recall much else about that day, and he's not certain when he learnt that they all had an older sister. Lynne's recollection was even vaguer — but then she was only three at the time. Lynne said that they never saw any pictures of Carole, even at their grandparents' house in Cardiff. 'I can't picture anything about what she was like; my grandparents never had photos up on the wall.'

They all agreed that it was very sad that there were no pictures of Carole on show, and they never even saw any of her wedding photographs. It's not just the thought that 'she was hidden away', as Ollie put it, but also that she was living so much closer to their grandparents than they were, and yet never appeared in their lives.

Davina discussed with them why they thought Carole was not talked about, and of course about the surprise that Carole was going to receive when she was told that she had a half-sister that she knew nothing about. Davina told them about Carole's memory of that day in 1960, and her recollection of Keith and Lynne, and what it would mean to her to know there was another sister whom she didn't meet. 'I was deliberately kept away from them that day,' said Ollie. 'I don't think Mum would have been too happy about the day.' Although it took them a while to figure all this out, it soon became clear that Ollie probably stayed with her grandparents that day.

Ironically, a few years later, maybe 1966, Ollie went to stay with her grandparents in

Cardiff for a few days. While she was there, she went to Roath Park with a friend. The friend pointed to a girl in the park and said, 'That's your sister.' Ollie could only see Carole's profile and, although curious, was too young and nervous to approach her — something she regrets.

Lynne explained, 'I think that's why we never went into it really, because it was part of Dad's life that had happened before and we weren't to bring it up. Not that we were ever told we couldn't bring it up, but it just wasn't the done thing.' They explained that their father was strict but he always provided for his family, that he was always nicely dressed and looked after himself well — and that he smelled of Old Spice. They felt an obligation to tell Carole as much as they could about him. While their mother was still alive, they would never have been able to look for Carole, and would have found it difficult to welcome her into their midst had she got in touch.

Now that both their parents were dead, it was sadly no longer possible for them to ask why things were as they had been, with Carole's life a closed book to their family. When their father died, his past was still not spoken about, because of their mother. Keith said, 'I feel a bit guilty that we didn't try to find Carole, to let her know our dad had died.'

They were all, however, very excited at the thought of Carole searching for them and at the possibility of meeting her. They all knew it would change the family dynamic a bit. Ollie, who as the eldest had always been the one to take charge, would have an older sister, and Keith joked that he would now be under the thumb of three sisters, not just two, but they wanted to welcome her into the family. Lynne, as the youngest, was the apple of her father's eye and grew up to be the nurturer of the family. This was obvious when Davina showed her the photograph of Carole she'd brought with her: she was so moved, immediately. Davina said the likeness between the two of them (and Ollie too) was startling. 'It's very amazing, it's me,' said Lynne. They could all see the family resemblance, that she was 'a Thomas', and Keith added, 'She's got Dad's nose, but it's straight — Dad's was broken, because of all the boxing.'

The final question was, of course, whether they would like to meet Carole, as she wanted to meet them. They all said yes, and Ollie added, 'Absolutely no hesitation. We do, very much.'

When Davina told Carole they'd found her siblings, she was immediately overcome by emotion. 'Really? Oh my gosh!' Tears sprang to her eyes, but she had to ask the question that had been eating away at her. 'Do they want to know me?' Davina nodded. 'Do they?' When Davina confirmed this, Carole cried with relief. She also wondered if they remembered the day she'd met them, fifty years ago. Davina explained that Keith remembered her, but Lynne was too young. 'She was little, quite tiny. Oh God, fancy remembering!' As she realised what this would mean, Carole started smiling.

Davina had a photograph to show her, of Keith and Lynne together. Carole was astonished at the strong family resemblance she saw. 'Oh my goodness! I look similar to them, even to the colour of her hair. It's amazing.' After explaining how thrilled they were at her getting in touch with them, Davina said that the *Long Lost Family* team had uncovered something else, 'quite big actually. You have another sister.'

Carole was momentarily lost for words, and could barely take the news in. 'Oh my lord.' Davina went on to tell her that Keith and Lynne's older sister, Ollie, had stayed away that day, and that 'she's no longer the oldest sister because of you'. Once she could take all this news in, Carole was very excited. 'I'm the eldest! Wow!' Seeing a photograph of

Ollie, she said, 'I'm shocked to start with, but thrilled to bits that I've got another sister. I am amazed, after all these years, that I've found them. Or you have — you've done it for me. Brilliant! Brilliant.'

The reunion

A short while later, Ollie, Keith and Lynne travelled down to Cardiff to meet Carole. Keith admitted to being really nervous, and Ollie declared her heart was 'thumping'. Lynne joined in, saying, 'My stomach's going. I've got butterflies. I can't wait to see her now.'

As they drove past the 'Welcome to Wales' sign on the motorway, Lynne said, 'Carole, we're here. Ollie, this is your last bit as the eldest sister.'

Ollie said she wasn't bothered by that, adding, 'I've said this dozens of times, I'm just going to pass all of it on to her.'

Drawing closer to Roath Park, Keith expressed the tension all three of them were feeling — 'I can't wait to see her, but what are we going to say?'

Wandering around the park where Keith and Lynne had met Carole fifty years before, very little of the surroundings were familiar to them. Only the boating lake itself and the swans swimming about on the water were sights they recalled.

Davina went to collect Carole to take her to the meeting. Holding her hand, Davina said, 'You're shaking.' Carole acknowledged this, and explained how very important this moment was going to be for her. 'This is real. I put names to the faces, I found out I had another sister, and I read the letter, and what she put at the bottom of it, about me being the big sister, that made me feel very emotional. I just hope it's all going to be okay and we're all going to be very close.'

The three siblings were sitting on a bench above the edge of the lake, and a very emotional Carole had to walk up a flight of steps to reach them. When she got there, they leapt off their seats and ran over to hug her.

There was so much for Carole to say, after such a long time — and to take in the fact that there was another sister alongside them was even more extraordinary for her. 'I didn't know anything about you,' she said to Ollie, 'until Davina gave me that photograph.' She was very moved and wanted to say everything at once, but admitted, 'There's such a lot, it's all up in my head, but I can't think.'

Ollie laughed and reassured her new big sister, 'We've plenty of time now. Have you got another fifty years to spare?'

They discussed their memories of that day fifty years before. 'That day we came down here,' said Keith, 'all I remember is being in the middle of the boating lake and Dad saying that Shirley Bassey used to live in one of those houses over there.'

Lynne explained that, 'We didn't even know who you were then. We weren't even told that you were our sister, just that we were going out for the day.'

The one absent from that day, Ollie, told Carole, 'I knew your name all along. I don't know how or when I knew — I feel like I always did.' They soon realised that the various memories they all had were going to need to be woven together carefully, as Carole had a clearer sense of the dates involved and her new siblings would need to clarify exactly when things they hazily recalled had actually taken place.

Carole also wanted to know what they'd known about her as they grew up. 'I was never sort of brought up in conversation?' She wondered whether or not anyone had talked about looking for her as the years passed.

Lynne explained: 'No. While Mum was still alive, it would have been too upsetting — and you said the same about your mum.' Carole agreed that she couldn't have looked for them until her mother died. Ollie added that there was no point in looking into why things had been the way they were: 'You can't really look back on the reasons why — you've just got to get on with right now.'

Carole thought she was right, and said, 'This is it. You've got to go forward, haven't you, and look to the future.'

Keith's contribution was to outline the immediate future: 'All I've thought of is what a big party we're going to have, to meet everybody.'

After the meeting, Ollie told the cameras, 'As soon as she came walking towards us, it didn't feel like she was a stranger. We had a connection. It was effortless. It's so obvious how happy Carole is about all this, and we're so happy for her.'

Carole was equally delighted. 'Keith caught hold of my hand as we were going down to the boat, and said, 'Come on now, big sister,' and I just thought, 'Oh, wow, yeah I am. I am a big sister.' It's lovely. Brilliant. Absolutely brilliant.'

After the programme

The evening after they'd filmed their reunion, they all went out to dinner together. Ollie had thoughtfully realised that one thing they would need to do for Carole was to provide her with some details about her father's life: 'Carole only had one photograph of Dad, taken on his wedding day. So we took lots of photos of him with us for her to look at.' They were able to tell her things about their life with him. He had been a strict father, but as he'd grown older, he'd turned into 'a bit of a softie, especially with his grandchildren'. They told her about his wartime experiences in the navy, how he had joined up when he was sixteen or seventeen, and then fought in the Far East. He had stayed in the navy after the war and had been a proficient boxer. He had travelled around the world — he'd mentioned South Africa, Durban in particular — and later on he had fought in the Korean War.

Ollie said to Carole that she had always wondered if this day would come along. Being the only one of the three who knew who Carole was, she had always planned to look into the story and see if she could find Carole one day — but of course she had had to wait until there was some free time for her to do so, which she thought would be when she retired. As she hadn't realised there was such an age gap between them, she was glad it had happened now. Already, though, she'd looked at the local census records, trying to work out from them where her relatives had lived, who they were connected to and where they might have moved to.

'The strangest thing out of it all,' said Ollie, 'is that Carole didn't know about me — and I was the only one that really knew about her.' Initially she had felt put out when she realised that Carole knew nothing about her, but almost as soon as she'd had that thought, it was pushed aside by the realisation that Carole was the one truly abandoned, not just by her father, but also by the other members of the family.

Quite why Carole hadn't seen more photographs of her dad before, and why none of them had seen photographs of Carole at their grandparents', was something none of them could clearly understand. It wasn't as if her grandparents had forgotten her. When Carole was small, her grandmother used to go and see her when Carole went to the Saturday morning pictures, but Carole was probably too young to understand why this had to be kept secret, so the visits were curtailed.

About the time the programme-makers made contact with Ollie, Lynne and Keith, they were midway through the process of going through their mother's papers, following her death a few months before. This gave an added dimension to the discussions they had with Carole. They came across their father's divorce papers, and photographs and letters exchanged between him and their mother from a few years before their marriage in July 1952. Their relationship had started with the two of them corresponding with each other while he was serving aboard ship.

Since their initial meetings, they have been down to Wales to celebrate Carole's sixty-fifth birthday. Keith brought Carole more photographs of their father and grandparents, while Ollie — who said, 'I had this thing of never knowing when Carole's birthday was when I was the only one who knew about her' — was at last able to choose the correct birthstone as a present. She also took her daughters and grandchildren to the party. Lynne bought Carole a present of porcelain figures of two sisters. Since then, Carole has been one of the family. Ollie and Keith will pick up the phone and call Carole as often as they call each other, although it is Lynne who speaks to Carole most often.

Since the programme was aired, a number of people have come up to Ollie and told her that they'd had similar experiences; two of them turned out to be people who belonged to the same club she did. One of them, who said to Ollie that she'd wept all the way through the programme, successfully found her brother. The other has yet to go ahead with her search, and Ollie is sympathetic to the daunting prospect she must feel is in front of her.

Ollie has been through more of the effects left by her mother, and she came across their father's wallet. In it, he had kept folded up neatly a small newspaper clipping, his mothers obituary, as it had appeared in the local paper. She had died in 1967 — quite a few years before — and he had been carrying it around all those years. Ollie was surprised by this, because she never thought of her father as sentimental. She is going to give the clipping to Carole next time she sees her.

Carole is delighted that she has finally met her sisters and brother. 'The missed years in my life have really been sad, because they could have been so full of family. They could have been so full of a lot more things. It would have been nice to have a family. It would have been nice. Maybe I can make up for it.'

Appendix

If you have been affected by any of the issues discussed in this book and would like either further information or to seek advice, please refer to the following websites, individuals or organisations for help and guidance:

Ariel Bruce

Website: www.arielbruce.com

An independent, registered social worker of twenty-five years' experience who specialises in tracing missing family members and offering intermediary services as an Adoption Support Agency. Based in London, Ariel carries out extensive work in the UK as well as in many countries worldwide. Using a global network of contacts and professional researchers, she has achieved a success rate in tracing people of over 90%. Ariel acted as the primary search consultant on *Long Lost Family*. A fee-paying service.

Adults Affected by Adoption: NORCAP

Website: www.norcap.org.uk

One of Britain's leading Adoption Support Agencies. Founded nearly thirty years ago, NORCAP focuses entirely on supporting adults affected by adoption. Providing a range of specialist services including operating the largest UK adoption contact register, giving guidance on how to locate lost relatives and a specialist intermediary service. A fee-paying service. NORCAP were consultants on *Long Lost Family*.

BAAF — The British Association for Adoption and Fostering

Website: www.baaf.org.uk

The BAAF supports, advises and campaigns for better outcomes for children in care, providing services to meet the needs of some of the UK's most vulnerable children and young people.

The Salvation Army Family Tracing Service

Website: www.salvationarmy.org.uk/familytracing

A people-finding agency.

The Adoption Contact Register

Website:
www.direct.gov.uk/en/
Governmentcitizensandrights/
Registeringlifeevents/Birthandadoptionrecords/
Adoptionrecords/DG_175603

The Adoption Contact Register puts adopted people and their birth relatives in touch with each other, if that is what they both wish. There are links via the website for the General Register Offices in Scotland and Northern Ireland.

Birthlink

Website: www.birthlink.org.uk

A registered charity offering a range of services for people separated by adoption with a Scottish connection.

Adoption Search Reunion

Website: www.adoptionsearchreunion.org.uk

A website for anyone thinking about searching for or making contact with birth and adopted relatives, or researching an adoption that took place in the UK.

After Adoption

Website: www.afteradoption.org.uk

A support agency for those whose lives are affected by adoption.

The Post-Adoption Centre

Website: www.postadoptioncentre.org.uk

A pre- and post-Adoption Support Agency since 1986.

The Genealogist

Website: www.thegenealogist.co.uk

A family history website. Its subscription service offers access to millions of records, including census, BMDs, parish records, directories, nonconformist records, PCC wills, peerage and heritage records, visitation records, electoral registers, newspapers and much more.

Genes Reunited

Website: www.genesreunited.co.uk

A family history website providing access to over eleven million family trees and birth, marriage and death indexes and census records through pay-per-view credits or subscription.

Find my Past

Website: www.findmypast.co.uk

A family history website established in 2003 providing subscription and pay-as-you-go access to over 750 million family history records, including birth, marriage and death indexes and complete censuses from between 1841 and 1911 for England and Wales, the current electoral roll, military records, passenger lists and parish records dating back 800 years.

Ancestry.co.uk

Website: www.ancestry.co.uk

A family history website offering members access to 895 million searchable UK family history records.

Birth, Marriage and Death indexes

It is possible to search the birth, marriage and

death indexes online for a subscription fee on websites such as www.ancestry.co.uk, www.findmypast.com and www.genesreunited.co.uk.

Electoral Roll

To search the current electoral roll for a fee: www.theukelectoral roll.co.uk. Also try www.tracesmart.co.uk or www.192.com.

Missing People

Website: www.missingpeople.org.uk

A charity offering support for people searching for a loved one who has gone missing or run away.

Scotland's People

Website: www.scotlandspeople.gov.uk

The official resource for Scottish family history, run as a partnership between the General Register Office for Scotland, the National Archives of Scotland and the Court of the Lord Lyon.

Acknowledgements

Wall to Wall would like to thank all the families we reunited as part of the series for their extraordinary trust, patience, courage and tenacity in allowing us to tell their remarkable, and very personal stories. Our thanks also to their extended families, whose support was and still is invaluable. We would particularly like to thank Ariel Bruce and AAA-NORCAP, whose expertise, advice and enormous skill in tracing people from every corner of the globe made many of these searches possible. There are many others whose help has been instrumental and to whom we extend our sincere thanks.

Publisher's Acknowledgements

The publishers would like to thank Humphrey Price, Wall to Wall's Annabel Borthwick, Julian Alexander from L.A.W. and copy-editor Juliana Foster for their invaluable assistance in creating this book. Also, thanks to Nicky Campbell for the book's foreword.

Other titles published by
The House of Ulverscroft:

TEA BY THE NURSERY FIRE

Noel Streatfeild

Emily Huckwell was born in a tiny Sussex village in the 1870s and went into domestic service in the Burton household before she was twelve, earning £5 a year. She began as a nursery maid, progressing to under nurse and then head nanny, looking after two generations of children. One of the children in her care was the father of Noel Streatfeild, the author of *Ballet Shoes* and among the best-loved children's writers of the twentieth century. Noel Streatfeild here tells Emily's story and with her characteristic warmth and intimacy creates a fascinating portrait of Victorian and Edwardian life above and below stairs.

CASPER THE COMMUTING CAT

Susan Finden

In Plymouth, in Devon, Casper became a national celebrity when newspapers ran the story of the black-and-white cat that regularly took the Number Three bus on eleven-mile journeys around his home town. Susan Finden, his owner, had wondered where her elusive pet was disappearing to each day, whilst Casper was brightening the lives of countless commuters on their journeys. Bus drivers were alerted to the fact that a small and furry passenger might board their vehicle and he became a mascot for the bus company. A very special cat, Casper and his remarkable story touched the lives of many people.

ONCE UPON A SECRET

Mimi Alford

In 1962, nineteen-year-old Mimi Beardsley began her internship in the White House press office, working for the Kennedy administration. She was soon presented to the President himself — and their affair began. But young Mimi, in her naivety, was emotionally unprepared: both for the impact on her of the President's charisma and power — and the feelings of isolation that followed. Then, after the President's tragic death in Dallas, she grieved in private and tried to start her life anew, only to find that her past would cast a long shadow — and ultimately destroy her relationship with the man she married.

BEAUTIFUL FOR EVER

Helen Rappaport

This is the true story of a woman who began life as a poor fish fryer in a disease-ridden, grubby corner of Victorian London. Madame Rachel had everything: a Mayfair address and the title of 'Purveyor to Her Majesty The Queen'. Her shop was full of exotic, expensive creams and potions. Her clientele were aristocratic, rich, gullible and came in their droves, lured by the promise of eternal beauty. What they found there was a con-woman and fraudster who made a career out of lies, treachery and the desperate hopes of women wanting to be 'beautiful for ever'.

NINETY DAYS

Bill Clegg

The goal is ninety: just ninety clean and sober days to loosen the hold of the addiction that caused Bill Clegg to lose everything. After seventy-three days in rehab, he returns to New York and attends two or three meetings each day. There, he befriends Asa — seemingly unshakeably sober — and Polly, struggling with her own cycle of recovery and relapse. When Clegg relapses for the first time, with only three days left, it turns his calendar back to day one. Hitting rock bottom is just the beginning of Bill Clegg's battle to reclaim his life.